ROOSIMINE
Knitted Socks

Spice up your sock knitting with this
easy-to-learn Estonian colorwork technique!

ROOSIMINE
Knitted Socks

Spice up your sock knitting with this easy-to-learn Estonian colorwork technique!

Stackpole Books
ESSEX, CONNECTICUT

STACKPOLE BOOKS
An imprint of The Globe Pequot Publishing Group, Inc.
64 South Main Street
Essex, CT 06426
www.globepequot.com

Copyright © 2026 The Globe Pequot Publishing Group, Inc.
Roosimine-Socken stricken © 2024 Edition Michael Fischer GmbH, Donnersbergstr. 7, 86859 Igling, Germany
This edition of *Roosimine-Socken stricken* first published in Germany by Edition Michael Fischer GmbH in 2024 is published by arrangement with Silke Bruenink Agency, Munich, Germany.

Cover design, book layout, and typesetting: Emilia Nedwidek
Photographs: © Corinna Teresa Brix, Munich, Germany (cover and lead photographs), © Sarah Prieur (step-by-step photographs), © Marcel Rotzoll, MRP Moving Images (author photograph)
Illustrations in chapter "Basics": Ina Langguth, Berlin, Germany
Text and photographs in chapter "Basics" (except p. 10, p. 22 bottom, p. 24, p. 35 bottom, pp. 38–40, pp. 42–44 top, pp. 45–48): Marisa Nöldeke
Project management and editing: Melanie Kowalski
Translation: Katharina Sokiran

All rights reserved. No part of this book may be reproduced in any form or by any electronic or mechanical means, including information storage and retrieval systems, without written permission from the publisher, except by a reviewer who may quote passages in a review.

The contents of this book are for personal use only. Patterns herein may be reproduced in limited quantities for such use. Any large-scale commercial reproduction is prohibited without the written consent of the publisher.

We have made every effort to ensure the accuracy and completeness of these instructions. We cannot, however, be responsible for human error, typographical mistakes, or variations in individual work.

British Library Cataloguing in Publication Information available

Library of Congress Cataloging-in-Publication Data available

ISBN 978-0-8117-7711-7 (paper : alk. paper)
ISBN 978-0-8117-7712-4 (electronic)

Printed in China

Foreword

As a knitter, I am always on the lookout for new challenges and particularly neat techniques to try out. When I first saw the Roosimine technique, which originated in Estonia, I knew immediately that I had to try it myself. Until then, I had only ever regarded floats as annoying things to be hidden on the back of your knitted fabric. Now, I am all the more enthusiastic about this traditional technique, which brings these floats to the front of the work and artfully uses them to give the knitted piece a very special appearance, that certain something.

The best thing about it is that the Roosimine technique is also a good introduction to knitted colorwork for beginners, as it is easier to knit than, for example, stranded colorwork or Intarsia.

Because socks always come in handy, I have designed a wide variety of sock patterns in the Roosimine style and prepared 18 sock projects with graphic, floral, and whimsical patterns in a wide range of sock yarns, from rustic tweed to fine cashmere.

And as I always encourage those using my patterns: Be creative! You can follow my instructions exactly, but you don't have to. Go ahead and combine cuffs, stitch patterns, and colors to create your very own, unique socks.

I wish for you to have as much fun knitting my sock patterns as I had designing them, and I will be very happy if you share your finished projects with me on Instagram @sapri_design under the hashtag #roosiminesockenstricken.

Sarah

Contents

Basics

Materials	10
Casting On	12
Basic Stitches	15
Knitting in the Round	22
Decreasing	26
Increasing	29
Picking Up Stitches	31
Binding Off	32
Finishing	34
Sock Knitting	35
Knitting Socks Toe-Up	42
Roosimine	45

Projects

Inna	52
Veli	56
Matis	60
Pinja	64
Kuldar	68
Sirja	72
Ivar	76
Ilme	80
Reelika	84
Veiko	88
Kalev	92
Kaisa	96
Taavi	100
Janek	104
Lisette	108
Anneli	112
Rain	116
Talvi	120
Acknowledgments	125
About the Author	127

Basics

Materials

YARN

Socks should preferably be knit from yarns marketed specifically as sock yarns. These yarns, thanks to their fiber content and special treatment, are durable, comfortable to wear, and machine washable. Traditionally, sock yarns consist mainly of virgin wool with a certain percentage (usually 20–30%) of polyamide (nylon) mixed in. The advantage of virgin wool is that it absorbs moisture and is breathable, which prevents unpleasant odors. Socks are subject to heavy friction, and the polyamide (nylon) fiber makes the yarn hard-wearing and retains the sock's shape.

Addition of other fibers such as silk or cashmere either gives the sock yarns a special luster or makes them particularly soft.

Sock yarns are available in different yarn weights. The most common are 4- and 6-ply yarns (fingering and DK weight).

KNITTING NEEDLES

Knitting needles come in a wide variety of materials such as wood, metal, and plastic. Which material you prefer to work with depends on your own preferences and also on how tightly or loosely you knit. Metal needles have a very smooth surface and are particularly suitable for knitters who knit very tightly. If you knit loosely, for example, bamboo needles with their somewhat grippier surface might work better for you.

Traditionally, socks are worked on double-pointed needle sets (DPNs) of 5 needles. In addition to regular-length DPNs, DPN sets of shorter needles around 6 in (15 cm) are also available, which are especially useful for smaller-diameter projects such as socks.

For those who prefer an alternative to a DPN set, there are various choices.

There are special DPN sets containing only 3 uniquely shaped needles, very short circulars intended specially for socks, or the option to work socks in the Magic Loop technique using a circular needle with a longer cord or two shorter circulars. Instructions for the different techniques for knitting in the round can be found on page 22.

ADDITIONAL TOOLS AND NOTIONS

Besides yarn and needles, you will also need a measuring tape, scissors, a blunt tapestry needle, and stitch markers. You can easily make your own stitch markers by knotting small pieces of contrasting color yarn into loops to place on your needles.

Casting On

LONG-TAIL CAST-ON

The classic long-tail cast-on is the most traditional and best-known method for casting on. It is especially easy to learn and master, which is a plus for beginners. This cast-on can be used for any stitch pattern and creates an especially sturdy and, at the same time, elastic edge.

PLEASE NOTE: Almost all cast-on methods start with a beginning slipknot (a.k.a. "beginning" or "sliding" loop).

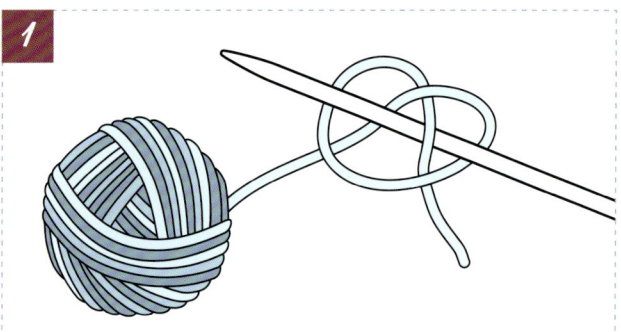

Start by placing a beginning slipknot on the right needle. The beginning tail should be three times as long as the intended width of the cast-on row—for thicker yarns somewhat more, for thinner yarns slightly less.

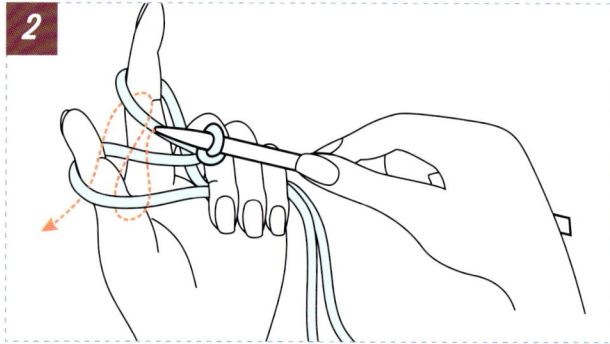

Lead the working yarn connected to the ball over your outstretched index finger, and the beginning tail over your thumb. Lead the needle first under the strand at your left thumb, then over the strand at your left index finger, and pull the needle through to the front, through both thumb strands, releasing the strand from your thumb to form a loop.

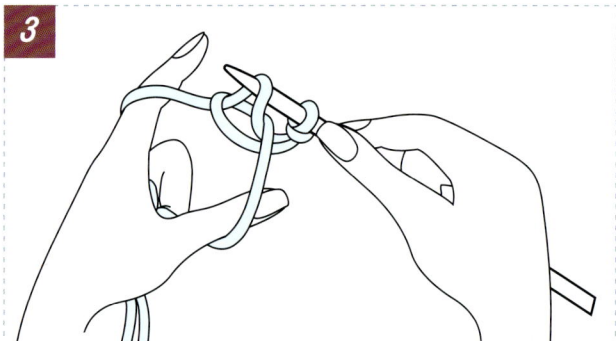

Tighten the loop on the needle, and place the strands onto the thumb and index finger as before. Repeat Steps 2 and 3 continuously.

Tip

Beginners tend to perform the long-tail cast-on especially tightly. If that happens to you, use two needles held parallel to each other to cast on instead of one needle—this creates a slightly looser cast-on. On the other hand, if your cast-on always comes out too loosely, use a needle one or two sizes smaller for the cast-on row.

ITALIAN CAST-ON FOR 1X1 RIBBING

The Italian cast-on is a method for the advanced knitter. It is one of the most used cast-on techniques for knitted items with ribbed cuffs, such as sweaters, cardigans, or socks. Here I will demonstrate with 1x1 ribbing, but similar techniques can be used to cast on knit and purl stitches for other ribbing variations. This technique creates an elastic and rounded edge for ribbing patterns. First the stitches must be wound onto the needles in a special manner and then the first 3 rows are also worked in a specific sequence for the best effect.

This method requires a little practice at first, but with a little experience and routine, the Italian cast-on will also come easily to you.

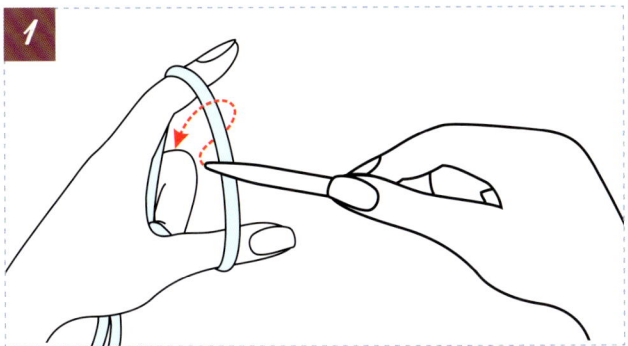

1 Lead the working yarn over the thumb and index finger, and place a loop onto the needle so that the strand coming from the index finger is located at the top and the strand coming from the thumb is located beneath it. Just as for a long-tail cast-on, here, too, leave a beginning tail about three times as long as the intended width of the cast-on row.

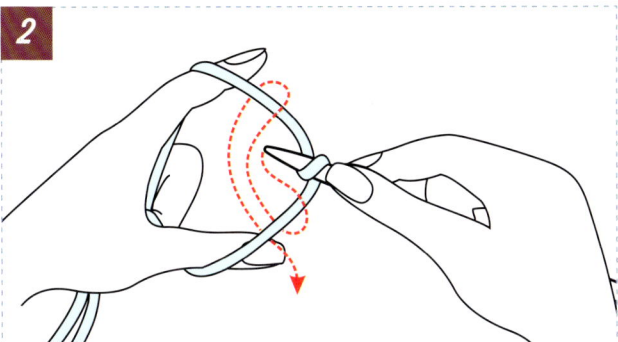

2 Now, pull the strand coming from the index finger through, under the strand coming from the thumb, and place it as a loop on the needle.

▶ continued on next page

3

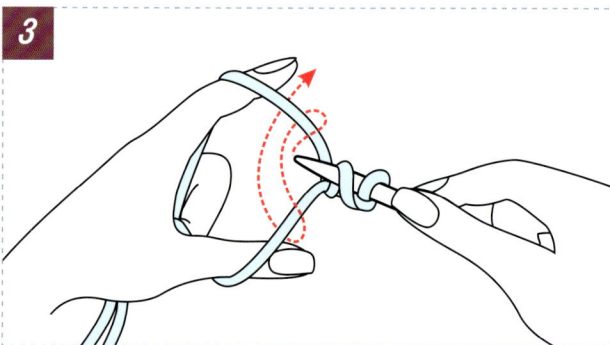

To cast on the next stitch, bring the needle over the index finger yarn, and then grab the thumb yarn and pull it up onto the needle.

4

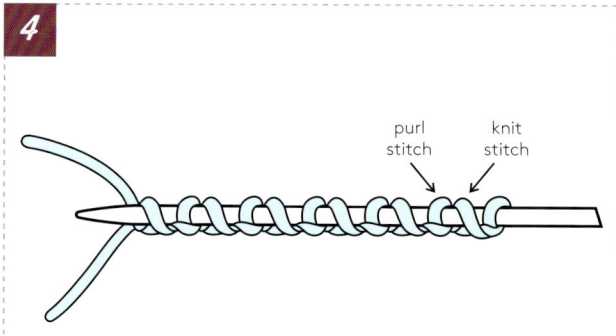

Repeat these steps alternately until the desired number of stitches are on the needle as loops. Make sure the new stitches don't twist. You'll then be able to clearly see the knit and purl stitches. However, in this foundation row, the *knit* stitches are still backward on the needle! They must therefore be worked through the back loop in the next row.

5

Work the first row by knitting the knit stitches through the back loop and slipping the purl stitches purlwise with yarn in front of work. In the next 3 rows, knit the knit stitches the regular way, and slip the purl stitches purlwise with yarn in front of work.

After this, work 1x1 ribbing as usual: Knit all knit stitches, and purl all purl stitches.

Tip

If you would like to have a particularly stretchy cuff for your socks, try the Italian cast-on.

Basic Stitches

KNIT STITCH

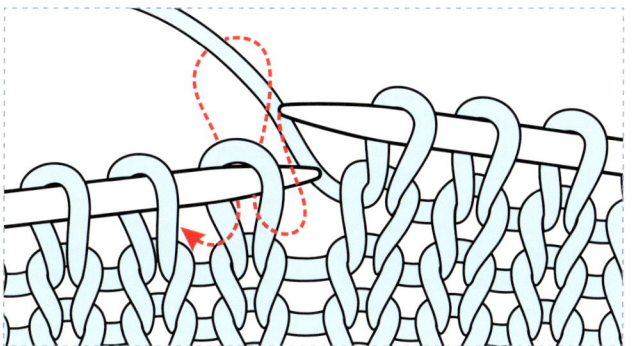

No matter which way and in which hand you hold the working yarn, how the knit stitch is worked always stays the same: Insert the right needle from front to back into the next stitch on the left needle. Grasp the working yarn from the top and pull it through the stitch. The newly formed stitch is sitting on the right needle. You can now let the old stitch slip off the left needle.

Check: The newly formed stitch is mounted on the needle with its right leg in front of and its left leg behind the needle.

PURL STITCH

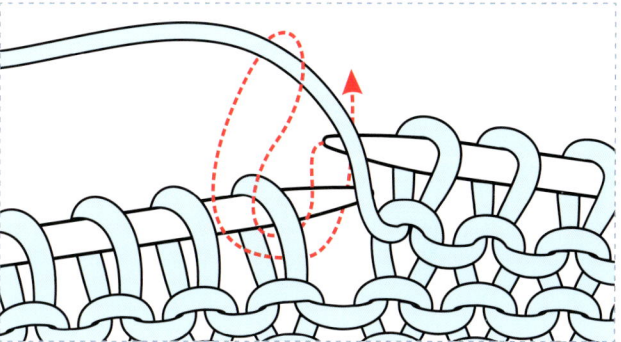

To work a purl stitch, hold the working yarn in front of work. Insert the right needle from right to left into the next stitch on the left needle. Place the working yarn from top to bottom around the needle, and pull the needle together with the working yarn through. Let the old stitch slip off the left needle.

Check: The newly formed stitch is mounted on the needle with its right leg in front of and its left leg behind the needle.

KNITTING STITCHES THROUGH THE BACK LOOP

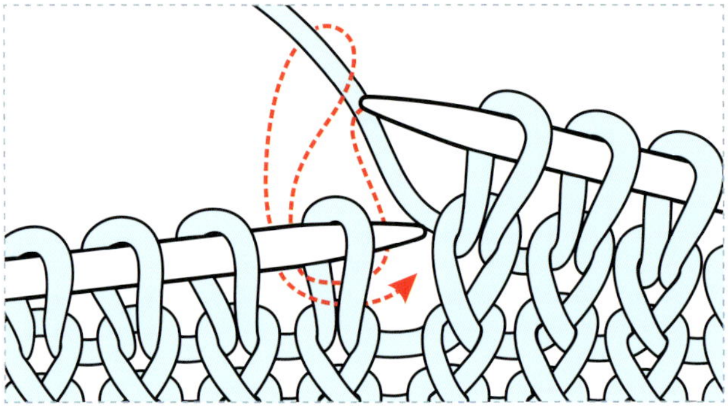

Hold the working yarn behind the needle. Then insert the right needle from right to left into the next stitch on the left needle, and pull the working yarn through. Stitches knitted through the back loop will appear with crossed legs in the knitted fabric.

PURLING STITCHES THROUGH THE BACK LOOP

To purl a stitch through the back loop, hold the working yarn in front of work as for working a regular purl stitch. Then insert the right needle from back to front into the back leg of the stitch, and pull the working yarn through.

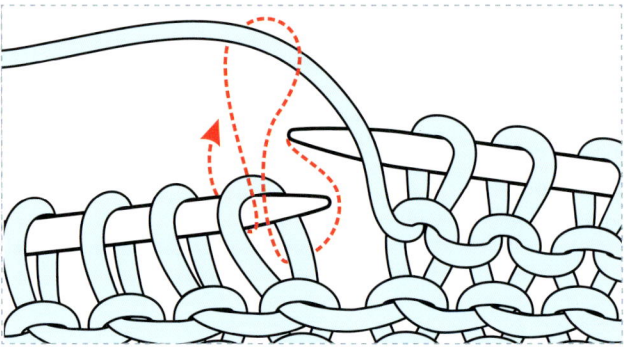

SLIPPED STITCHES

Slipped stitches are used in some types of decreases, but also in so-called slipped-stitch patterns. Slipped-stitch patterns worked in two colors are often called mosaic knitting. When slipping a stitch, the needle is inserted into the stitch either knitwise or purlwise, then the stitch is, without being worked, placed onto the right needle. The working yarn is either held in back of work or in front of it, depending on the pattern.

PLEASE NOTE: A popular misconception relates to the position of the working yarn while slipping the stitch. The working yarn should not be placed on the needle, which would automatically create an increase. When slipping a stitch, the working yarn is always carried along either in front of or behind the slipped stitch.

SLIPPING A STITCH KNITWISE

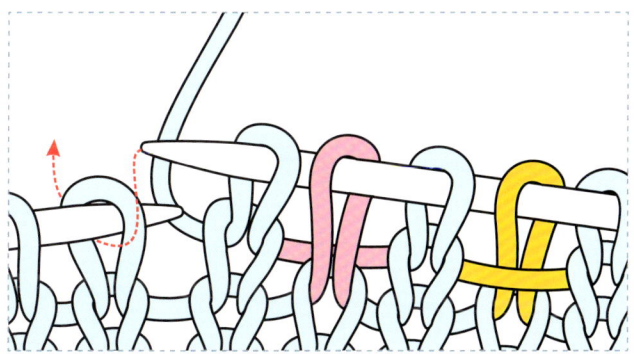

To slip a stitch knitwise, insert the right needle into the stitch as if to knit, and place it onto the right needle without actually working it. The stitch highlighted in yellow and the stitch highlighted in pink have both been slipped, one with the working yarn in front of work and the other with the working yarn behind work. You can see that they have been slipped knitwise by the fact that the right leg of the stitch is now located behind the needle.

SLIPPING A STITCH PURLWISE

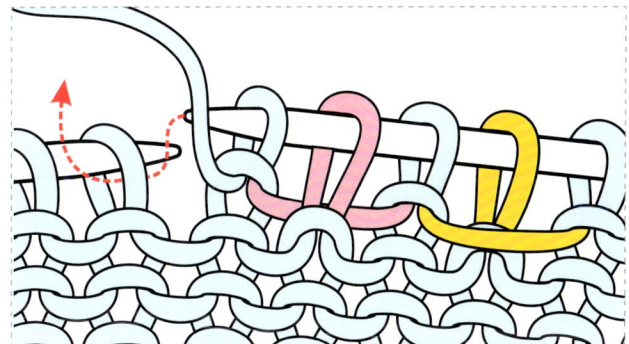

To slip a stitch purlwise, insert the right needle into the stitch as if to purl, and place it onto the right needle without actually working it. Here, too, the stitch highlighted in yellow and the stitch highlighted in pink have both been slipped, with the working yarn in front of or behind work respectively. You can see that they have been slipped purlwise by the fact that the right leg of the stitch is now located in front of the needle.

Basic Stitches 17

RECOGNIZING STITCHES

Over time, you will get the hang of recognizing the stitches on the needle and in the knitted fabric. But especially at the beginning, it's easy to lose track of things. Did you just work a knit or a purl stitch?

Knit stitches can be recognized by the little "V" below the needle and also in the knitted fabric. Purl stitches lie across the row like a beam. For all stitches worked the regular way, the right leg of the stitch is always located in front of the needle, and the left leg of the stitch behind the needle. In comparison, there are stitches worked through the back loop (twisted), which you learned about on page 16.

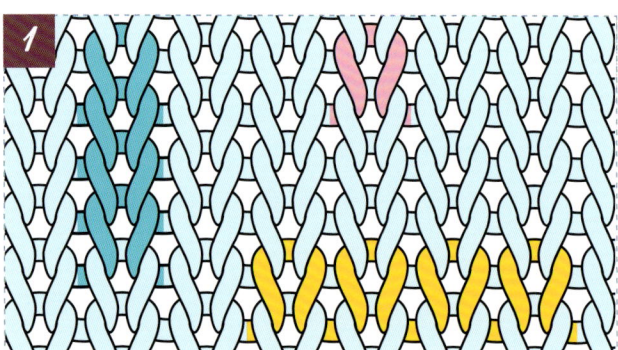

Stockinette stitch: All stitches on the right side of the fabric are knitted. An individual knit stitch has been highlighted in pink. Four worked rows are highlighted in blue. Highlighted in yellow are four adjacent knit stitches.

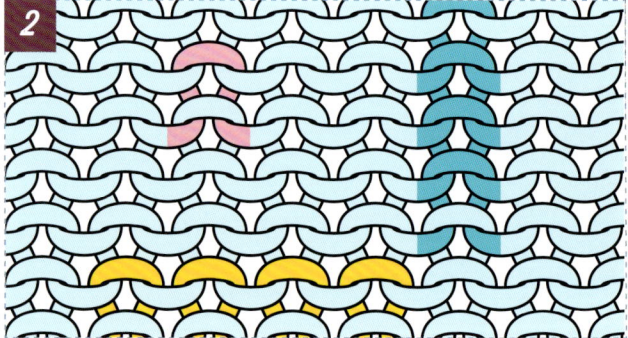

Reverse stockinette stitch (stockinette stitch as viewed from the wrong side of the fabric): This illustration shows the wrong side of stockinette fabric. Knit stitches appear on the wrong side as purl stitches.

Garter stitch: Here, all stitches in all rows (right side and wrong side) are always knitted. This lets the rows appear on the same side of the fabric alternatingly as knit and as purl stitches. The blue stitch appears as a purl stitch on the other side of the fabric here. In the row above it, the stitch highlighted in pink, viewed from the other side of the fabric, is a knit stitch. Blue and pink show two rows accordingly. Highlighted in yellow are two rows and four adjacent stitches.

PLEASE NOTE: Knit stitches appear on the wrong side of the knitted fabric as purl stitches, purl stitches on the other hand as knit stitches. Once you have mastered this concept, it will be easy to distinguish between knit and purl stitches on the needles.

STOCKINETTE STITCH IN ROWS

When working knitted pieces in stockinette stitch, stitches in right-side rows, meaning on the public side or outward-facing side of the knitted item, are always knitted. In wrong-side rows, on the nonpublic or inward-facing side of the knitted item, the stitches are purled. They will appear as knit stitches when the fabric is viewed from the right side.

>
> Circular needles are not just for knitting in the round. They are also helpful for larger projects in back-and-forth rows, where the large number of stitches can be held on the cord rather than heavily on long needles.

SHORT-ROW SHAPING

To work short rows means to work only part of the stitches, stopping before the actual end of the row. Work is turned before the end of the row has been reached and continued on the other side in the opposite direction.

The particular challenge when knitting short rows is to hide the turning spot as invisibly as possible within the knitted fabric.

PLEASE NOTE: If the turn happens in a purl row, the first stitch after having turned (in this case, a knit stitch) will be slipped purlwise, too (with working yarn in front of work). After this, the working yarn is pulled to the back, above the stitch.

Basic Stitches

GERMAN SHORT ROWS WITH DOUBLE STITCH

In this method, the stitch in the turning spot is worked as a double stitch by pulling the working yarn to the back and tightening it until the stitch sits on the needle with both legs. Later, both legs of the double stitch are either knitted or purled together as one and count as one stitch.

This method is especially well suited for knitted pieces subjected to wear and tear, since the turning spot is practically invisible even when the knitted fabric is stretched considerably.

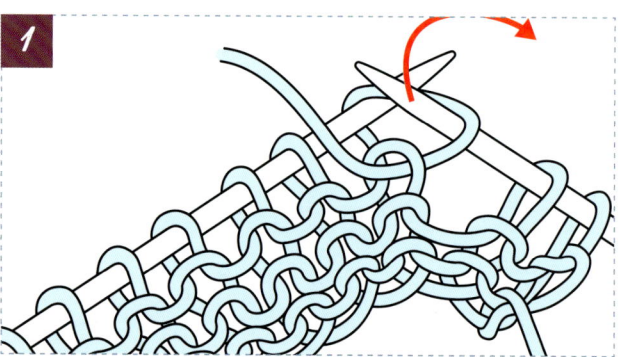

After having turned, slip the first stitch purlwise with working yarn in front of work.

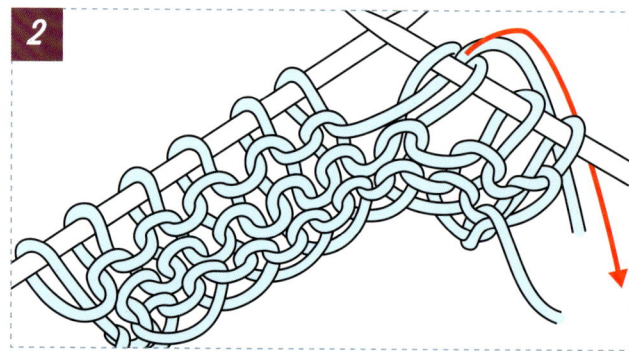

Then pull the working yarn from front to back over the right needle and over the just-worked stitch so that both legs of the stitch are on the needle.

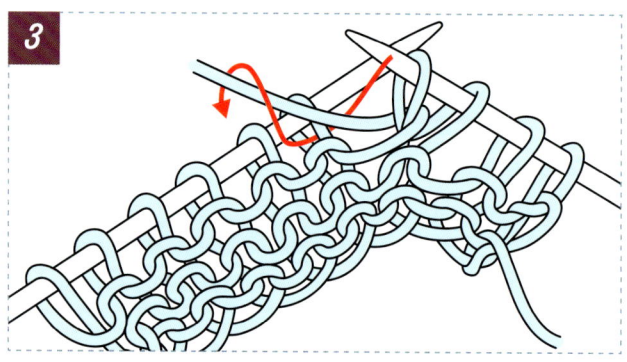

Continue the row as instructed.

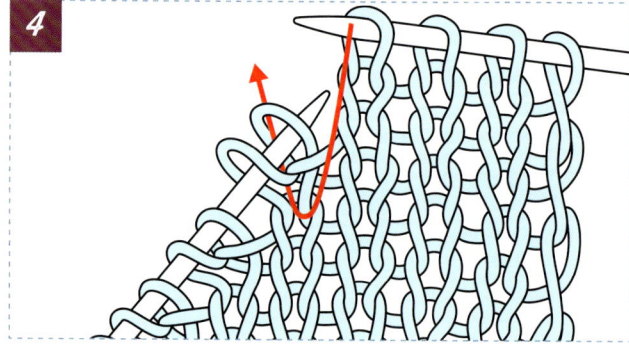

On the next row, when you reach the turning stitch, work both legs of the double stitch together as one.

COLOR CHANGE IN TURNED ROWS

Changing colors is a common stumbling block, even for experienced knitters. Often the working yarn in the old color is needlessly cut where the change takes place. When working stripes in lots of different colors, having to weave in all the ends at the end can very quickly ruin the fun for you. Instead, leave the yarn in the old color attached, and carry it upward at the outside edge of work. Decide for yourself over how many rows you find this strategy agreeable. This is a matter of personal taste, and there are no set rules for this.

When working narrow stripes in two alternating colors, the unused color can be carried up at the edge.

This way, you don't have to break the yarn at every color change and can save yourself the trouble of having to weave in countless tails at the end of the project.

The carried strand is, of course, slightly visible at the edge. Always crossing the strands over each other in the same direction will make the color changes less noticeable in the finished project.

Basic Stitches

Knitting in the Round

USING A DPN SET WITH 4 OR 5 NEEDLES

The required stitch count is distributed evenly onto 3 or 4 needles, while the 4th or 5th needle is used to work the stitches.

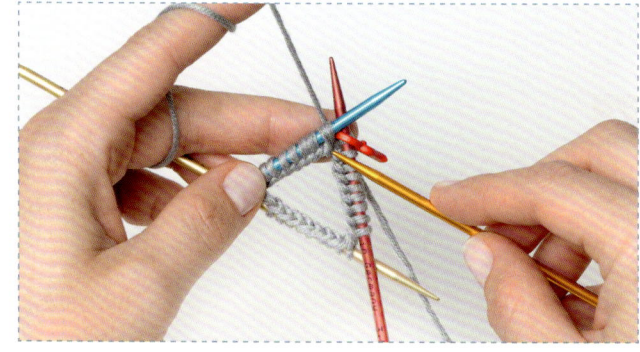

USING A DPN SET WITH 3 NEEDLES

The required stitch count is distributed evenly onto 2 needles, while the 3rd needle is used to work the stitches.

USING A CIRCULAR NEEDLE

For casting on stitches using the Magic Loop method, the circular needle should have a length of 40 in (100 cm). Cast on the required number of stitches onto the circular needle. At the exact midpoint of the stitches, pull out a loop of the cord of the circular needle between the stitches.

Push half of the stitches onto the tip of the left needle, while the other half of the stitches stays on the cord. The pulled-out cord loop is located between the two sections of stitches. Position the tip of the right needle pointing left as shown, with the cord loop to the right of the needle, and use the tip of the right needle to work the stitches sitting on the left needle.

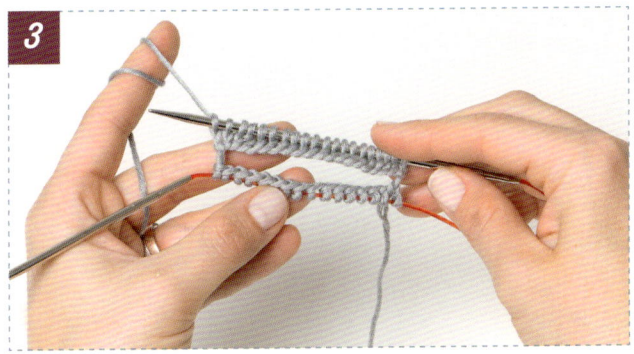

Here, all of the stitches from the left needle have been knitted onto the right.

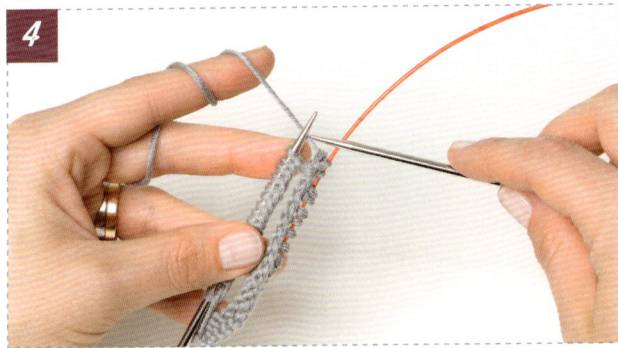

Turn work, slide the unworked stitches onto the tip of the left needle, and slide the already worked half of the stitches onto the cord. Use the tip of the right needle to work the stitches sitting on the left needle.

Knitting in the Round 23

USING TWO CIRCULAR NEEDLES

For knitting in the round using two circular needles, each circular should be at least 24 in (60 cm) long.

Cast on the required number of stitches onto two circular needles, equally distributed. Keep each half on its own circular needle. Each half of the stitches will only be worked using the tips of the needle on whose cord the stitches are sitting, while the other stitches are resting on the cord of the other needle. The beginning of the round is located between the needles, where the beginning tail is attached.

Slide the stitches of the section in the back onto the cord of the second circular needle, with both needle tips hanging down. Slide the stitches of the section in the front onto the tip of the circular, and work them off using the unused needle tip attached to the same cord.

Slide the already worked stitches onto the cord, then turn work. Move the stitches on the second circular onto one of the needle tips of that circular, and work them off using the unused needle tip attached to the same cord.

Slide the already worked stitches onto the cord, then turn work. Continue working in this manner. While one half of the stitches is being worked, the other half is resting on the cord of the unused circular.

PLEASE NOTE: No matter which method you use, please keep in mind that the beginning of the round for all socks in this book is located in the middle of the heel stitches. Please always mark the beginning of the round with a stitch marker and, if needed, redistribute the stitches on the needles. For both methods using circular needles, it is convenient to place the beginning of the round in the middle of a needle.

All instructions in this book have been written with a traditional DPN set in mind. If you are using a different method for knitting in the round, you will need to divide the stitches into four sections and mark with stitch markers, at least while working the heel and during the toe decreases.

COLOR CHANGE IN THE ROUND

When changing color in the round, unsightly color steps ("jogs") occur in the spot where the old round ends and the new one starts, which you can minimize using the following trick.

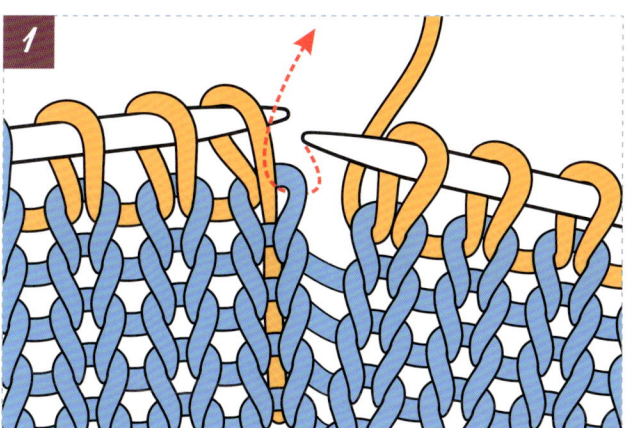

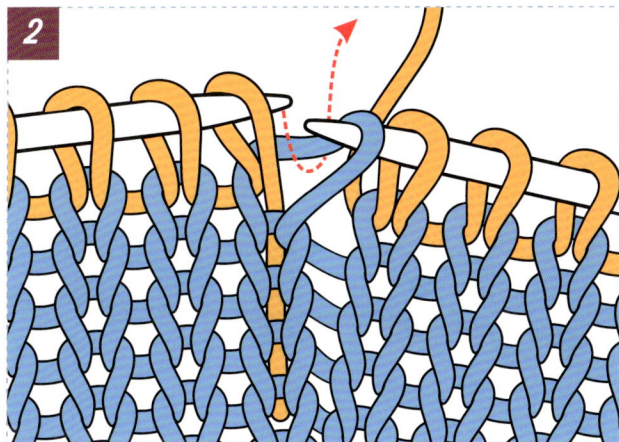

Work the first round in the new color. At the beginning of the second round, insert the right needle tip into the stitch from the previous round located directly below the first stitch of the round, and lift this stitch onto the left needle.

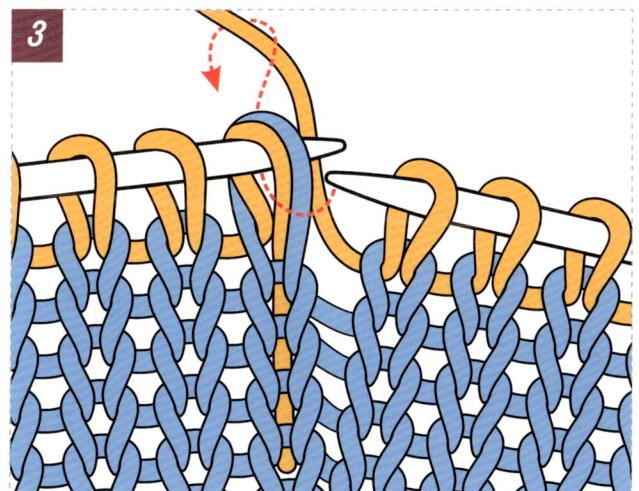

PLEASE NOTE: When changing colors in the round, the strand in the unused color can be carried upward in back of work. In this case, even broader stripes with fewer color changes can be worked. Cross the strands at the beginning of every round to prevent loose floats on the wrong side.

Then knit it together with the first stitch of the second round.

Decreasing

RIGHT-LEANING DECREASE

Knitting 2 Stitches Together (k2tog)

This decrease looks as if it were leaning to the right, which is why it is used at the left edge of knitted pieces.

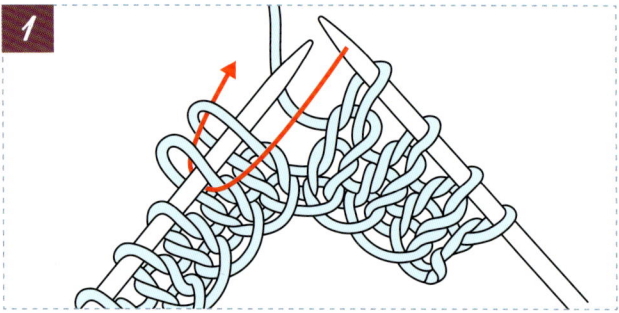

Insert the right needle from front to back first into the second stitch on the left needle and, after that, into the first stitch.

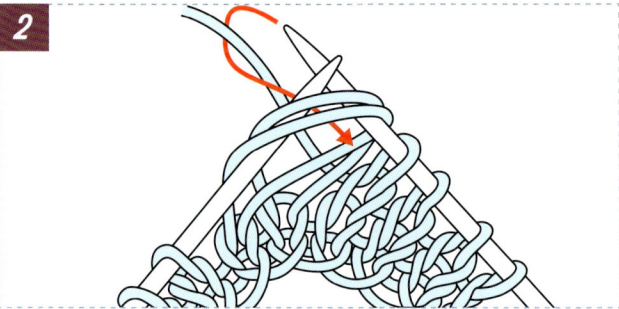

Pull the working yarn through as if to knit.

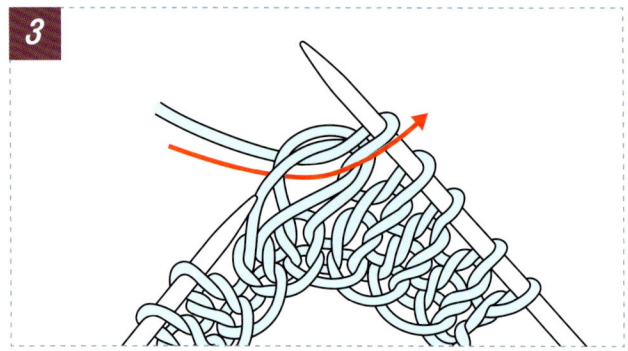

Let both stitches slip off of the left needle.

Three or more stitches can be knitted together in the same way as well.

> **Tip**
>
> When decreasing next to an edge, use the following rule: The decrease should always run parallel to the edge. When working a decrease at the left edge of a knitted piece, the edge itself will move to the right. Therefore, you should work a right-leaning decrease here and work a left-leaning decrease at the right edge of the piece accordingly.

LEFT-LEANING DECREASES

This decrease looks as if it were leaning to the left, and is therefore worked at the right edge of knitted pieces.

Knitting 2 Stitches Together Through the Back Loop (k2tog-tbl)

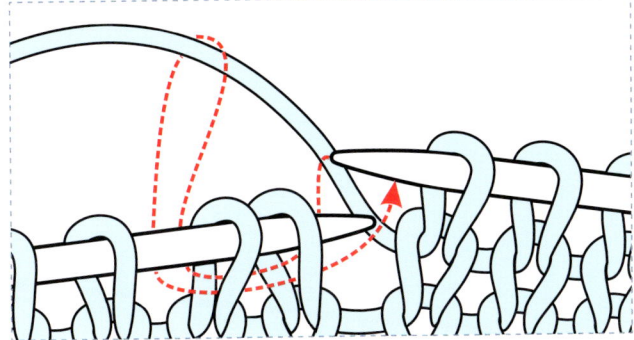

Insert the right needle from right to left into the next two stitches on the left needle together and knit them through the back loop.

PLEASE NOTE: When this decrease is worked on the wrong side of the fabric, it appears right-leaning on the right side of the fabric. It is initially worked at the left edge of the knitted piece on the wrong side, but after the piece has been turned to the right side, on that side of the knitted fabric, it will appear leaning to the left.

Slip, Slip, Knit (ssk)

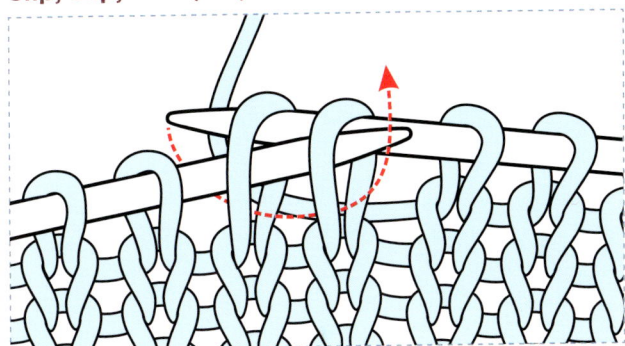

Insert the right needle into the next stitch as if to knit and slip this stitch to the right needle, then slip the following stitch to the right needle the same way. Return the two stitches to the left needle one after the other so that they are mounted on the needle with the other leg in front, as shown in the illustration. Now, knit both stitches together through the back loop.

Slip, Knit, Pass the Slipped Stitch Over (skp)

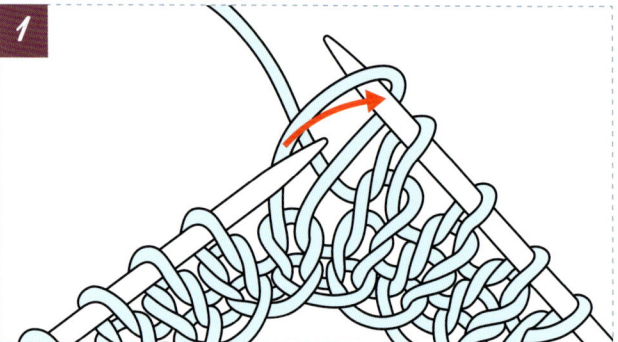

Slip the first stitch as if to knit.

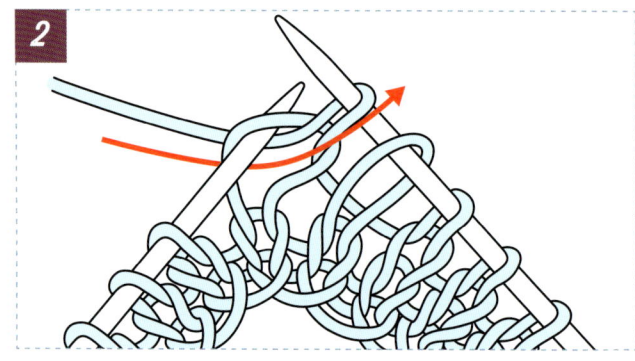

Knit the next stitch.

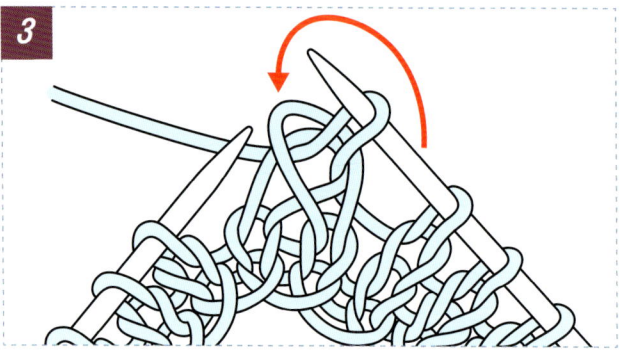

Pass the previously slipped stitch over the knitted one from right to left and off the needle.

Increasing

MAKE 1 LEFT (M1L)

Increases from the bar between stitches are especially popular since they blend in very well with stockinette stitch fabric. They are often worked to the right and left of one or more center stitches. In this case, they are worked mirror-inverted, once right- and once left-leaning.

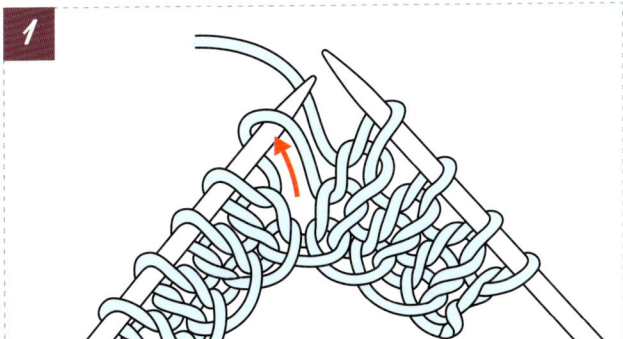

Insert the left needle from front to back under the bar between stitches on the tips of the right and left needles.

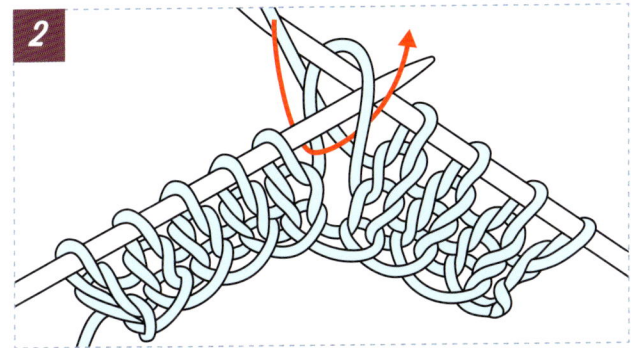

Knit the bar between stitches through the back loop (twisted) . . .

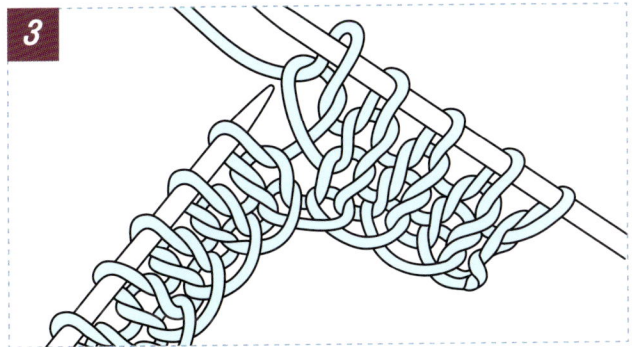

. . . and let it slip off of the left needle.

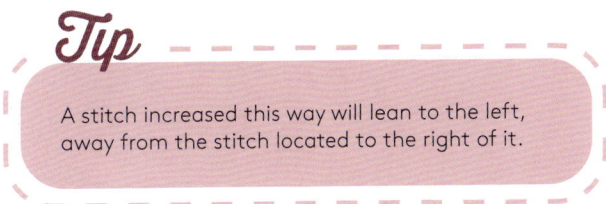

Tip

A stitch increased this way will lean to the left, away from the stitch located to the right of it.

MAKE 1 RIGHT (M1R)

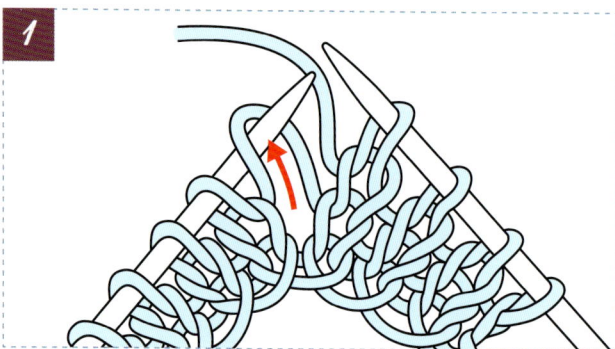

Insert the left needle from back to front under the bar between stitches on the tips of the right and left needles.

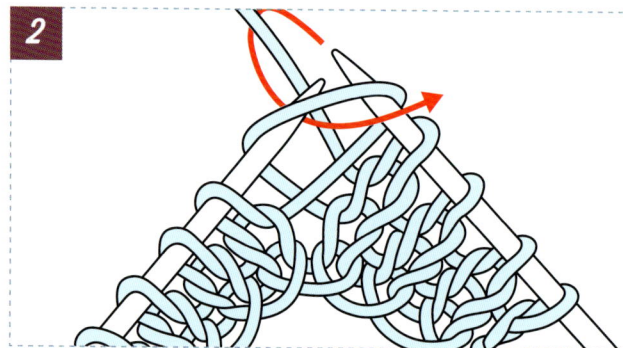

Knit this bar between stitches the regular way (not twisted) . . .

. . . and let it slip off of the left needle.

MNEMONIC: To remember which way a stitch increased from the bar between stitches will lean, use this mnemonic: "I LEFT the FRONT door open" (a bar picked up from front to back produces a left-leaning increase), and "I will be RIGHT BACK" (a bar picked up from back to front produces a right-leaning increase).

Picking Up Stitches

Stitches are picked up in different ways, depending on how the edge of the knitted piece is constructed. Each type of edge has special characteristics that must be considered when picking up. Stitches can be picked up all around a knitted piece: They can be picked from horizontal edges (cast-on or bound-off edges), vertical edges (side edges), or bias or curved edges, as well as directly from within the knitted fabric.

Stitches are picked up on the right side (public side) of the knitted fabric, working from right to left.

If you have already knitted a few items or gauge swatches in stockinette stitch or garter stitch, you might have noticed that the stitches have different height-to-width ratios.

PICKING UP STITCHES FROM A SIDE EDGE

When stitches need to be picked up from a side edge, the above-mentioned height-to-width ratio has to be considered: Stitches in knitted fabric are most often more wide than tall.

If one stitch were to be picked up from every row, there would be too many stitches in the picked-up part. This would create excess fabric.

Tip

If the knitted fabric puckers or ripples after the stitches have been picked up, no matter on which edge it happened, too few or too many stitches have been picked up. In this case, the pick-up ratio (i.e., the ratio of picked-up stitches to the length of the edge from which they are picked up) needs to be adjusted.

The ratio between stitch width and stitch height depends on the stitch pattern. Individual stitches in stockinette stitch fabric appear narrower than stitches worked in garter stitch.

Cable patterns often constrict considerably, so their height-to-width ratio can be quite different from that of pieces worked in stockinette stitch.

Tip

When the picked-up part will be worked in a contrasting color, stitches need first to be picked up in the old color, changing to the new color before the next row. This creates a neater and less noticeable transition.

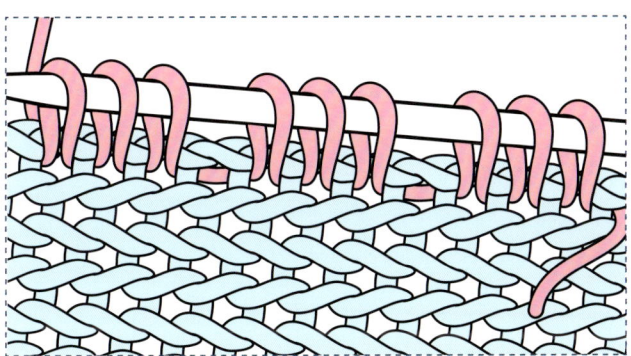

PLEASE NOTE: The ratio between stitches and rows for pieces worked in garter stitch fabric is approximately 1:2; for pieces worked in stockinette stitch approximately 3:4. The exact ratio can be determined through a gauge swatch.

Binding Off

BINDING OFF BY PASSING OVER

Binding off by passing over is the easiest of all methods for binding off. This bind-off can be used equally well with knit and purl stitches.

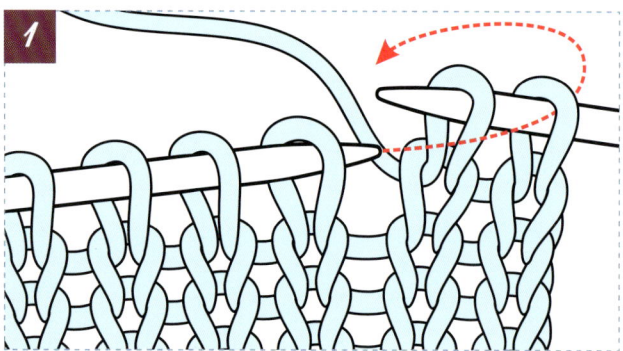

Knit the first two stitches one after another, then insert the left needle from left to right into the first one of the two previously worked stitches.

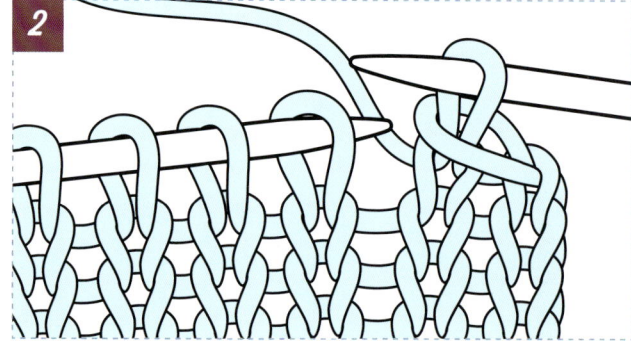

Pass this stitch over the stitch to the left of it and off of the needle. One stitch has been bound off. Knit the next stitch, and again, pass the stitch to the right of it over the stitch and off the needle.

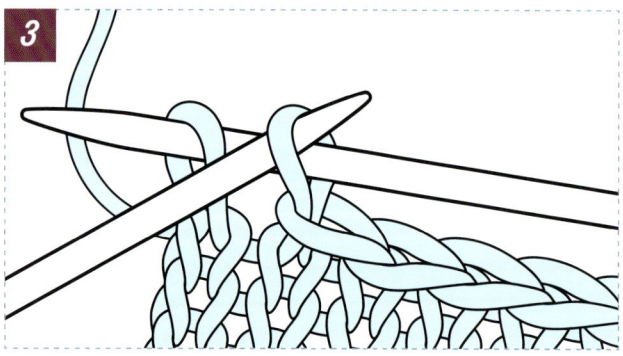

Repeat these steps to the end of the row. Then break the working yarn, leaving an end of 4 in (10 cm) or longer, and pull the tail through the last stitch. You will weave this end in later.

PLEASE NOTE: Binding off in purl or in pattern is done the same way. Stitches are worked as they appear, that is, knit stitches are knit and purl stitches are purled.

Finishing

WEAVING IN ENDS

At the end of the knitting project, all ends resulting from having joined new colors or skeins have to be hidden. Hiding ends neatly is made much easier if the tails from cast-on, bound-off, or joining new yarn are not too short but have been left at least 4 in (10 cm) long.

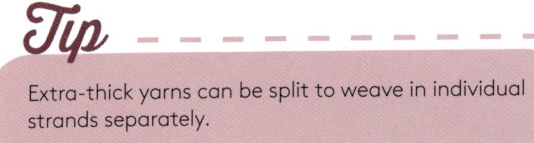

Tip

Extra-thick yarns can be split to weave in individual strands separately.

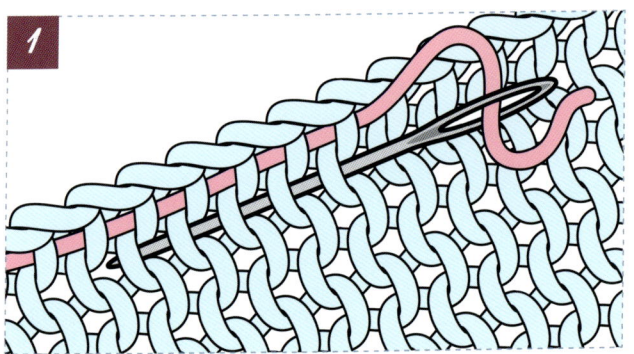

Where possible, weave in the tails along the edge of the knitted piece.

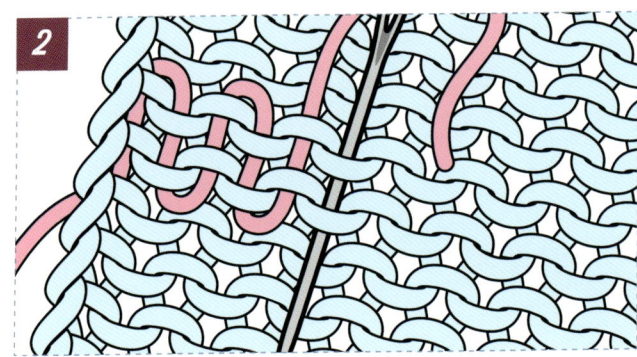

Should it become necessary to weave in ends within the knitted fabric, first thread the tail through to the wrong side of the fabric. Once there, weave in the end in a meandering path.

WASHING AND BLOCKING

Either wash the knitted piece in the wool cycle of your washing machine, or let it soak in lukewarm water in the sink. With very bright colors, stay nearby to monitor the process, and be prepared to remove the piece from the water immediately if the colors bleed. Then, rinse the knitted piece thoroughly, press out the water without wringing, and roll the piece in a towel. Continue to press out moisture. Spread out the piece on a blocking mat, and pull it into shape. If specific blocked measurements are given in the instructions, take them into account. Pin the knitted piece to the blocking surface using blocking pins. Depending on the stitch pattern or desired special effects, you can use blocking wires threaded through the edge stitches to stretch the knitted piece. Afterward, leave the work to dry flat.

PLEASE NOTE: Make sure to use rustproof pins for blocking. Special T-pins available in knitting supply stores are the best choice.

KNITTING WITH MULTIPLE COLORS: COUNTING CHARTS FOR STRANDED COLORWORK

When working stranded colorwork using multiple colors, instructions will often contain a colorwork chart that visually represents the colorwork pattern. Each box in the chart stands for a stitch in one color, each row of boxes for a row or round. When working in the round, all rows are read from right to left. When working in rows, right-side rows are read from right to left, wrong-side rows from left to right.

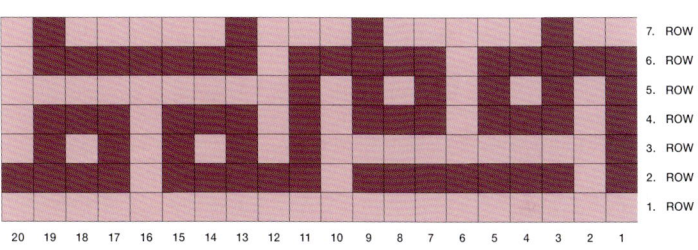

Sock Knitting

CUFF

Sock cuffs are worked in stretchy stitch patterns to ensure that the sock stays securely on the leg and to prevent it from sliding down. Besides the traditional ribbing choices, you can also get creative and opt for decorative ribbing patterns, such as variations with cables.

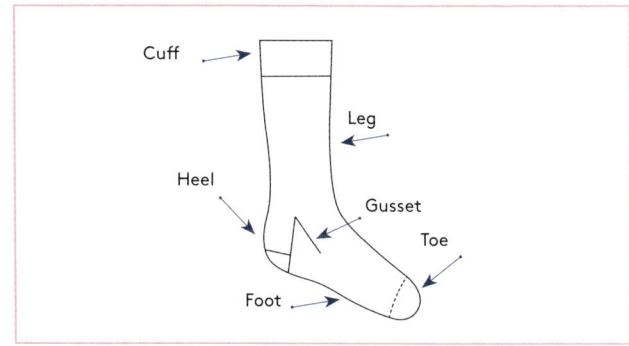

LEG

The cuff is followed by the leg section of the sock, which most often is worked even in the round, without increases or decreases. When the stitch pattern allows for it, the leg length can be adjusted as desired.

HEEL

The heel constitutes the most important part of the sock; this is what determines whether the finished sock fits well. Instep height and heel width are key to a perfect fit. In this book, three different heel constructions are used, which are explained in detail on the following pages.

Boomerang Heel

This heel is for feet with a low instep and any foot width. Have a look at how this heel type looks knitted up in the project Ilme on page 80.

This heel is shaped with short rows. It is less suitable for self-patterning yarns, since after half of the heel has been completed, two rounds are worked over all of the stitches, which disrupts the pattern. As with an afterthought heel, this heel does not have a gusset, which means the fit is not optimal.

The heel stitches are divided into sections according to the numbers for the appropriate size in the sock table on page 41. The starting point is the center of the middle section of heel stitches.

Row 1 (RS): Knit to end of heel stitch section. Turn work.

Row 2 (WS): Pull out a double stitch, purl to end of heel stitch section. Turn work.

Row 3 (RS): Pull out a double stitch, knit to previous double stitch, turn work.

Row 4 (WS): Pull out a double stitch, purl to previous double stitch, turn work.

Repeat Rows 3 and 4 continuously until all stitches of the side sections have been placed on the needles as double stitches.

Intermittent rounds: Knit two rounds over all stitches (top of foot and heel), while, in the first round, working both legs of each double stitch together as one. Place the stitches on the top of the foot on hold again, then work the second part of the heel over all heel stitches. Starting point is the center of the heel stitch section.

Row 1 (RS): Knit the stitches of the center section and the first stitch of the side section, turn work.

Row 2 (WS): Pull out a double stitch, purl the stitches of the center section and the first stitch of the side section, turn work.

Row 3 (RS): Pull out a double stitch. Knit the stitches of the center section, knit both legs of the double stitch together as one, knit the next stitch of the side section, turn work.

Row 4 (WS): Pull out a double stitch, purl the stitches of the center section, purl both legs of the double stitch together as one, purl the next stitch of the side section, turn work.

Repeat Rows 3 and 4 continuously until the two outermost stitches of the side section have been placed on the needles as double stitches. Work half of a right-side row, ending in the center of the heel section, then resume working in the round over all stitches.

Turned Heel

This heel is for feet with a high instep and a slim foot width. Have a look at how this heel type looks knitted up in project Kalev on page 92.

The turned heel is the classic among the heel types. It consists of three parts: the heel flap is worked first in turned rows, then the heel turn is worked by knitting the appropriate stitches together, followed by picking up new stitches from the resulting side edge and working a wedge-shaped gusset for a better fit of the whole sock. In preparation for the heel flap, stitches are divided into sections according to the stitch counts stated in the sock table (page 41) for the size worked, then the listed number of rows is worked, and then the heel turn is worked over the stated number of stitches as follows:

Row 1 (RS): Knit to the last stitch of the middle section. Slip this last stitch and the first stitch of the side section one after another as if to knit, place them back on the left needle, and knit them together through the back loop.

Row 2 (WS): Slip 1 stitch purlwise with working yarn in front of work, purl to the last stitch of the middle section. Purl this last stitch of the middle section together with the first stitch of the side section.

Row 3 (RS): Slip 1 stitch purlwise with working yarn in front of work, knit to the last stitch of the middle section. Slip this last stitch and the first stitch of the side section one after another as if to knit, place them back on the left needle, and knit them together through the back loop.

Repeat Rows 2 and 3 continuously until all stitches of the side sections have been used up. Working a right-side row, end in the center of the heel section.

Resume working in the round over all stitches, while in the first round picking up and knitting stitches at a rate of 1 stitch picked up from every 2 rows along the side edges of the heel flap. The additional stitches created this way for more room in the instep will be decreased again during gusset decreases so that the midsection of the foot will again be worked over the initially cast-on stitch count.

After having picked up the stitches, work one round over all stitches, ending in the center of the heel section.

Gusset decreases: Knit to the last 3 stitches of the sole section, then knit 2 stitches together. Work the stitches on the top of the foot in knit (or in other stitch pattern as listed). Knit the first one of the sole stitches, then slip 2 stitches individually as if to knit, place them back on the left needle, and knit them together through the back loop. Continue in knit to the center of the heel stitches.

Repeat these decreases in every 2nd or 3rd round, depending on instep height, until all extra stitches have been decreased and you have reached the initial stitch count again.

Depending on whether decreases are worked in every 2nd or 3rd round, the gusset will turn out steeper or shallower.

Fleegle Heel

This heel is for feet with a high instep and a medium foot width. Have a look at how this heel type looks knitted up in the project Veli on page 56.

The Fleegle heel looks similar to a turned heel. Extra room in the heel area is created through a large wedge that is shaped by increases in the center of the heel. In contrast to other heels, this part of the heel is continued to be worked in the round. The sole portion of the heel (heel step wedge) is then subsequently shaped by another wedge with short-row shaping.

Heel Flap Wedge

For the heel flap wedge, divide the total stitch count into two equal parts: the stitches on the top of the foot and the heel stitches. Work the heel flap wedge in the round over the heel stitches, and the stitches on the top of the foot in pattern if applicable.

Unlike other heels, the starting point is not in the center of the heel stitch section but rather at the beginning of needle 4.

Round 1: Knit to 1 stitch before the center of the heel, place marker 1, make 1 left from the bar between stitches (Photo 1), knit 2 stitches, make 1 right from the bar between stitches (Photo 2), place marker 2. Knit all remaining stitches.

Round 2: Work all stitches as they appear (knit the knits and purl the purls), slipping markers when you encounter them.

Round 3: Knit to marker 1, slip marker, make 1 left from the bar between stitches, knit to marker 2, make 1 right from the bar between stitches, slip marker. Knit the remaining stitches.

Round 4: Work all stitches as they appear (knit the knits and purl the purls), slip marker (Photo 3).

Repeat Rounds 3 and 4 continuously until the number of stitches increased on each side is 1 stitch fewer than the stitch count for half the heel stitch section. Remove marker. The end of the round is again before needle 4 (Photo 4 and Photo 5).

Heel Step Wedge

The heel step wedge is shaped with short rows.

Knit half of the heel stitches. The starting point is located in the center of the heel stitches.

Row 1 (RS): Ssk, knit 1, turn work.

Row 2 (WS): Slip the first stitch purlwise, purl 1, p2tog, purl 1, turn work.

Row 3 (RS): Slip the first stitch purlwise, knit 2, ssk, knit 1, turn work.

Row 4 (WS): Slip the first stitch purlwise, purl 3, p2tog, purl 1, turn work.

Repeat Rows 3 and 4 continuously, always slipping the first stitch and working to 1 stitch before the resulting gap. Knit this stitch together with the following stitch, then knit 1 (Photo 1). The wedge widens in every row by 1 stitch until all heel stitches have been worked. At that point, the initial stitch count has been reached again, and the foot is continued in the round over all stitches (Photo 2 and Photo 3).

FOOT

After the heel has been completed, the foot is continued in the round again. The sock is divided into two parts: the instep (top of the foot) and the sole (bottom of the foot).

TOE DECREASES

Toe decreases are the final steps of a sock; in this part, too, there are different options and shapes for ending the sock. The length of the toe decrease section can vary along with its shape, which can be pointed, round, or blunt.

All designs in this book are worked with paired banded toe decreases since this type does not affect the colorwork or stitch pattern.

Paired Banded Toe Decreases

Round 1: On needles 1 and 3, knit to the last 3 stitches on needle, k2tog, k1; and on needles 2 and 4, knit 1, skp, knit to end of needle.

Rounds 2–3: Knit all stitches.

Round 4: Work as Round 1.

Round 5: Knit all stitches.

Round 6: Work as Round 1.

Round 7: Knit all stitches.

Round 8: Work as Round 1.

From here on, repeat the decreases from Round 1 in every round until 2 stitches remain on each needle, for a total of 8 stitches on all needles together.

Break the working yarn, thread the tail into a tapestry needle, then thread it through all 8 stitches two times, thread the tail through to the inside of the sock, pull taut, and weave in the end on the wrong side.

SOCK TABLES

SIZE(S)	W5½/6	W7/8	W9/9½, M7/7½	W11/12, M8½/9	M10/11
Stitch count total	60	60	64	64	68
Stitch count per needle	15	15	16	16	17
Stitch count in heel	30	30	32	32	34
# of sts to be picked up from each heel flap edge	15	15	16	16	17
Total foot length in inches (cm)	9.75 (24.5)	10 (25.5)	10.5 (27)	11.25 (28.5)	11.5 (29.5)

PLEASE NOTE: The Correct Sock Size

Every foot is different. These sock tables provide a good estimate for the stitch count and the foot length to be worked. You may nevertheless have to make adjustments for your individual size. Try on the sock every now and then while knitting to check width and length.

TURNED HEEL

# of rows in heel flap	30	30	32	32	34
Stitch distribution for heel flap	10/10/10	10/10/10	10/12/10	10/12/10	11/12/11
# of sts to be picked up from each heel flap edge	15	15	16	16	17

BOOMERANG HEEL

Stitch distribution for heel flap	10/10/10	10/10/10	10/12/10	10/12/10	11/12/11

LENGTH OF PAIRED BANDED TOE DECREASES IN INCHES (CM)	2 (5)	2 (5)	2.25 (5.5)	2.25 (5.5)	2.5 (6)
Length of foot before toe decreases in inches (cm)	7.75 (19.5)	8 (20.5)	8.25 (21.5)	9 (23)	9.25 (23.5)
Decrease sequence					
In every 4th round	once	once	once	once	once
In every 3rd round	2 times	2 times	2 times	2 times	2 times
In every other round	3 times	3 times	3 times	3 times	4 times
In every round	6 times	6 times	7 times	7 times	7 times

Knitting Socks Toe-Up

Socks can be worked not only from the cuff down to the toe but also the other way around, from the toe up, beginning at the toe, on to the heel, and finishing with the cuff.

CAST-ON

Blunt Banded Toe with Long-Tail Cast-On for Toe-Up Socks

Required stitch count for the blunt banded toe:

Sizes W5½–W8: 8 stitches

Sizes W9/9½–M11: 10 stitches

Total stitch count (stitch count overall/per needle):

Sizes W5½–W8: 60/15 stitches

Sizes W9/9½–M8½/9: 64/16 stitches

Sizes M10–M11: 68/17 stitches

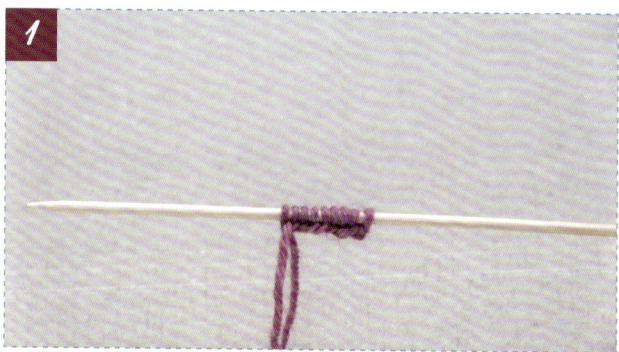

For the long-tail cast-on, place the working yarn over the thumb and the short tail over the index finger (note that this placement is opposite of the standard long-tail cast-on). Holding the working yarn this way, cast on one stitch more than the listed stitch count for the blunt banded toe.

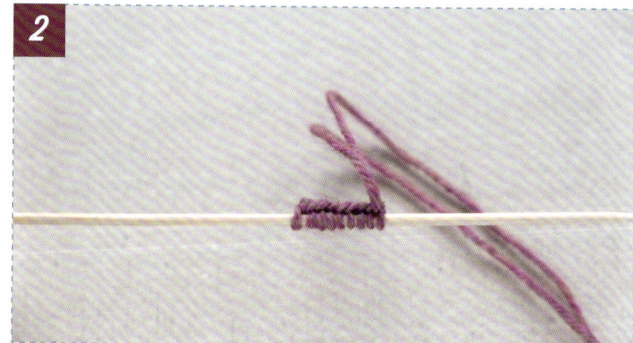

Do not turn work, rotating it by 180 degrees instead. The cast-on edge is now located at the top.

Using needle 2, pick up and knit 1 stitch each between all of the stitches, until the correct stitch count for the blunt banded toe is on this needle.

Rotate work by 180 degrees. Knit all stitches except for the last one. Let the last stitch slip off of the left needle, and pull the working yarn taut. Mark the beginning of the round for future increases.

Rotate work by 180 degrees. Distribute the stitches evenly onto 4 DPNs. The numbering of the needles after the stitch marker is as follows: needle 4, needle 1, needle 2, and needle 3.

Work stockinette stitch in the round, increasing in every other round as follows: On needles 1 and 3, before the last stitch on this needle, make 1 left from the bar between stitches, on needles 2 and 4, after the first stitch, make 1 right from the bar between stitches. Continue in this manner until the total required stitch count has been cast on.

Knitting Socks Toe-Up

HEEL

For toe-up socks, all diagonal seam heels, such as the boomerang heel, can be used, since heels of this type consist of identical top and bottom parts.

CUFF

Toe-up socks are bound off after having worked the cuff. This means it is very important to bind off loosely. An especially neat and elastic final round can be created using the Italian sewn bind-off method.

Italian Sewn Bind-Off

Begin by working two rounds as follows: In the first round, knit the knit stitches and slip the purl stitches purlwise with working yarn in front of work. In the second round, purl the purl stitches and slip the knit stitches knitwise with the working yarn behind work. After this, use sewn bind-off to bind off the stitches.

To work the sewn bind-off, thread the yarn tail into a tapestry needle and insert the needle first from right to left through the selvedge stitch and pull the working yarn taut. If the stitch after the selvedge stitch is a knit stitch, insert the needle once more from right to left through this stitch. Now, begin the sewn bind-off in pairs of one purl and one knit stitch each. Repeat Steps 1–3, below, especially carefully until all stitches are bound off:

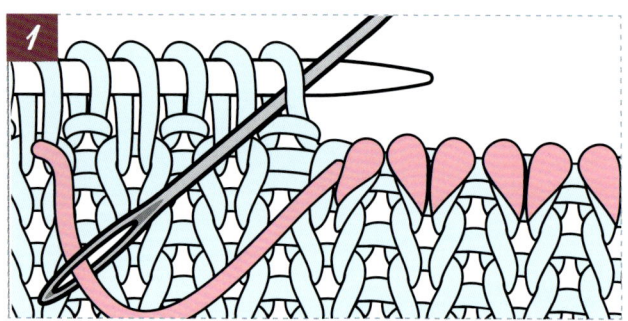

Thread the needle from left to right through the purl stitch.

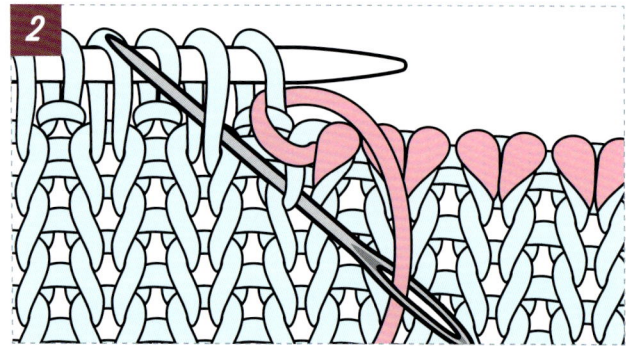

Thread the needle from right to left first through the preceding knit stitch, and then through the second stitch on the knitting needle (which is also a knit stitch).

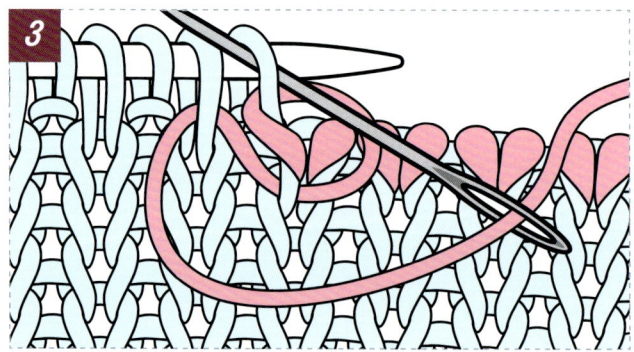

Thread the yarn from right to left once more through the first purl stitch. Now, let both sewn-off stitches slip off of the left needle.

Roosimine

The Roosimine technique is an Estonian Intarsia technique. The special feature of this technique is that strands in a contrasting color are not knitted but, instead, carried in front of the knitted fabric as visible floats. These floats appear on the public side of the knitted piece as a contrasting pattern on top of the base fabric in main color. Embellishments added this way create the effect of embroidery.

Literally translated, Roosimine means "to decorate with roses." In Estonia, the Roosimine technique is traditionally used predominantly on gloves and stockings. This way of knitting is called "Roosimine," and the finished knitted piece is called "Roositud."

The Roosimine technique can be applied to nearly any project that is knitted in the round. While care has to be taken here, too, to ensure even tensioning, the Roosimine technique is often easier to work for beginners than other techniques using multiple colors, such as stranded colorwork or Intarsia.

How to Work Patterns in the Roosimine Technique

The yarn for the embellishment can be held either single or double.

Round 1

Lead the long end of the yarn used for the embellishment through to the front of work between the needles.

Now, using the main color, work the number of stitches that are supposed to be spanned by the colorwork motif (in the pictured example, 2 stitches). Make sure that the working yarn in main color is always kept above the embellishment strand in contrasting color.

▶ continued on next page

Lead the strand in motif color through to the back of work again between the needle tips, and, using the main color, work the following stitches up to the next motif section.

Repeat Steps 1–3 to continue the motif.

If the pattern is worked all through the whole round, repeat Steps 1–3 continuously round after round. Make sure to use an even, not-too-tight tension.

If the pattern is worked over part of the round only, you will follow different directions for every other round to avoid too long floats on the wrong side.

Round 2

Step 1: Work up to the spot where the pattern begins. Lead the strand in motif color over the left needle to the front of work . . .

. . . and between the needles to the back of work again, creating a large loop in front of work.

46 Basics

Work the number of stitches that are supposed to be spanned by the colorwork motif, then lead the whole loop over and between the needles to the back of the work again.

Work the following stitches up to the next section of the motif. To work the pattern in the next spot, lead the complete loop over and between the needles to the front of work again, and continue the pattern in this manner.

When you have finished working the pattern, continue, working a few more stitches in main color, then place the knitted piece in front of you so the wrong side of the fabric is visible.

▶ continued on next page

To hide the loop, gently pull at the long end of the embellishment strand in contrasting color.

For the next round, the working yarn is again located on the right side of the knitted fabric. Work, using the embellishment strand in contrasting color alternatingly as described for Round 1 and Round 2 to avoid excessively long floats.

> **Tip**
> Make sure to work at an even tension. If you are working too tightly, the pattern will constrict, while working too loosely can cause unsightly gaps.

> **Tip**
> Especially when working with multiple colors, washing the finished piece will greatly affect the stitch definition. If you are not yet completely satisfied with your work, treat your knitted piece to a relaxing bath, and then leave it to dry, spread out horizontally.

SPECIAL CONSIDERATIONS WHEN READING COLORWORK CHARTS FOR ROOSIMINE WORK

Colorwork charts and knitting charts are read from top to bottom and from right to left. Each box in the chart corresponds to one stitch in the actual knitting (see page 35). The special feature of the Roosimine technique is that the thread is carried horizontally over several stitches. A bar in the colorwork chart indicates, therefore, that the embellishment strand in contrasting color needs to be placed horizontally over exactly this number of stitches.

ABBREVIATIONS

approx. = approximately
cn = cable needle
CO = cast on
DPN(s) = double-pointed needles
k = knit
k2tog = knit 2 stitches together (1 st decreased)
m = stitch marker
p = purl
p2tog = purl 2 stitches together (1 st decreased)
pm = place marker
skp = slip, knit, pass the slipped stitch over (1 st decreased)
ssk = slip, slip, knit (1 st decreased)
st(s) = stitch(es)
-tbl = through the back loop
-tog = (knit or purl # of sts) together
yo(s) = yarn over(s)

DIFFICULTY LEVEL

■ Easy

■
■ Intermediate

■
■ Advanced
■

Projects

Inna

SIZES

W5½/6 (W7/8, W9/9½ [M7/7½], W11/12 [M8½/9], M10/11)

MATERIALS

Lana Grossa Meilenweit 100 Merino Extrafine: 75% Merino wool, 25% polyamide/nylon; 459 yd (420 m) per 3.5 oz (100 g)

- Gray-Blue 2420: 1 skein
- Lilac 2435: 1 skein
- Pink 2454: 1 skein
- Reseda Green 2430: 1 skein

DPN set in US size 2 (2.5–3.0 mm) (or other preferred needle type, see page 10)

Stitch markers

Tapestry needle

Scissors

GAUGE

In stockinette stitch with US size 2 needles (2.5–3.0 mm):

28 sts and 40 rows = 4 x 4 in (10 x 10 cm)

BASIC PATTERN

STOCKINETTE STITCH

In rows: Knit on RS, purl on WS.
In rounds: Knit all stitches in all rounds.

CUFF RIBBING

2x2 ribbing: *Knit 2, purl 2*, repeat from * to * continuously.

CONSTRUCTION

The sock is worked from the cuff down, featuring a boomerang heel and paired banded toe decreases. The colorwork pattern on the leg is worked with two strands of yarn held together.

INSTRUCTIONS

CUFF

CO 60 (60/64/64/68) sts in Gray-Blue, distribute sts evenly onto 4 DPNs [= 15 (15/16/16/17) sts per needle], and join to work in the round.

Work 10 rounds (= 1 in [2.5 cm]) in cuff ribbing.

LEG

Change color to Lilac and work 3 rounds in stockinette stitch.

LEFT SOCK

In Round 4, k33 (33/36/36/38), pm, k9, pm, k18 (18/19/19/21).

RIGHT SOCK

In Round 4, k18 (18/19/19/21), pm, k9, pm, k33 (33/36/36/38).

Work 49 rnds in stockinette stitch, working the pattern over 9 sts widthwise between the markers with two strands of Pink and Reseda Green, respectively, held together.

Work 5 rnds in stockinette stitch, then remove the markers.

HEEL

Work a boomerang heel in stockinette stitch in Gray-Blue over the 30 (30/32/32/34) sts of needles 4 and 1 according to Basic instructions (see page 36), in intermittent rounds, work the 30 (30/32/32/34) sts of needles 2 and 3 in Lilac.

> **Tip**
>
> If frequent color changes and having to weave in lots of ends do not appeal to you, you can for ease of work just substitute a turned heel according to Basic instructions in Gray-Blue (see page 37).

FOOT

For the foot, change color to Lilac again, and work stockinette stitch in the round.

TOE DECREASES

After having worked 6.25 (7/7.5/8/8.75) in [16 (17.5/19/20.5/22) cm] (measured from the middle of the heel), change color to Gray-Blue, and begin working paired banded toe decreases (see page 40).

FINISHING

Weave in all ends.

COLORWORK CHART

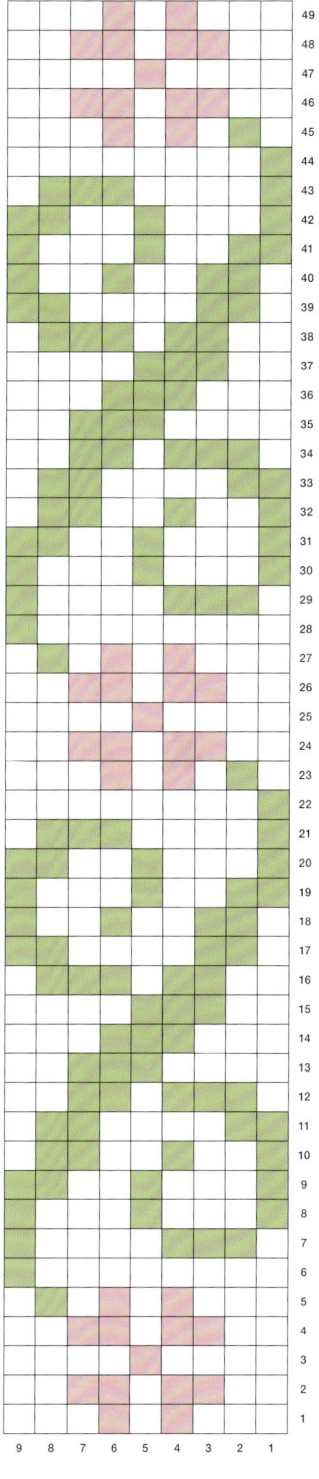

Inna 55

Veli

SIZES
W5½/6 (W7/8, W9/9½ [M7/7½], W11/12 [M8½/9], M10/11)

MATERIALS
Lana Grossa Meilenweit 50 Cashmere: 70% superwash wool, 25% polyamide/nylon, 5% cashmere; 230 yd (210 m) per 1.8 oz (50 g)
- Fuchsia 52: 2 skeins

Lana Grossa Meilenweit 100: 80% wool, 20% polyamide/nylon; 459 yd (420 m) per 3.5 oz (100 g)
- Petrol 1371: 1 skein

DPN set in US size 2 (2.5–3.0 mm) (or other preferred needle type, see page 10)

Stitch markers

Tapestry needle

Scissors

GAUGE
In stockinette stitch with US size 2 needles (2.5–3.0 mm):
30 sts and 40 rows = 4 x 4 in (10 x 10 cm)

BASIC PATTERN
STOCKINETTE STITCH
In rows: Knit on RS, purl on WS.
In rounds: Knit all stitches in all rounds.

CUFF RIBBING
1x1 twisted ribbing: *Knit 1 through the back loop, purl 1*, repeat from * to * continuously.

CONSTRUCTION
The sock is worked from the cuff down featuring twisted cuff ribbing, a Fleegle heel, and paired banded toe decreases. The colorwork motif is on the front of the sock.

INSTRUCTIONS

CUFF

CO 60 (60/64/64/68) sts in Fuchsia, distribute sts evenly onto 4 DPNs [= 15 (15/16/16/17) sts per needle], and join to work in the round.

Work 20 rounds [= 2 in (5 cm)] in cuff ribbing.

LEG

Work 9 rounds in stockinette stitch.

In Round 10, k20 (20/22/22/24), pm, k21, pm, k19 (19/21/21/23).

Work 75 (75/75/75/89) rnds in stockinette stitch, working the pattern with one strand of yarn in Petrol over the 21 sts between the markers according to colorwork rounds listed below.

After having worked approx. 5.75 in (14.5 cm) (measured from cast-on edge), begin working a Fleegle heel according to Basic instructions (see page 38) over the 30 (30/32/32/34) sts of needles 4 and 1, continuing the pattern on the front of the sock.

SIZES W5½/6, W7/8, W9/9½ [M7/7½], W11/12 [M8½/9]

Rounds 1–25: Work Rounds 1–25 of Colorwork Chart A.

Rounds 26–67: Work Rounds 12–25 of Colorwork Chart A three times in all.

Rounds 68–75: Work Rounds 1–8 of Colorwork Chart B.

SIZE M10/11

Rounds 1–25: Work Rounds 1–25 of Colorwork Chart A.

Rounds 26–81: Work Rounds 12–25 of Colorwork Chart A four times in all.

Rounds 82–89: Work Rounds 1–8 of Colorwork Chart B.

FOOT

Work in stockinette stitch, and complete the 75 (75/75/75/89) rounds of the colorwork pattern. Then, continue in stockinette stitch.

TOE DECREASES

After having worked 6.25 (7/7.5/8/8.75) in [16 (17.5/19/20.5/22) cm] (measured from middle of heel), begin working banded paired toe decreases (see page 40).

FINISHING

Weave in all ends.

COLORWORK CHART A

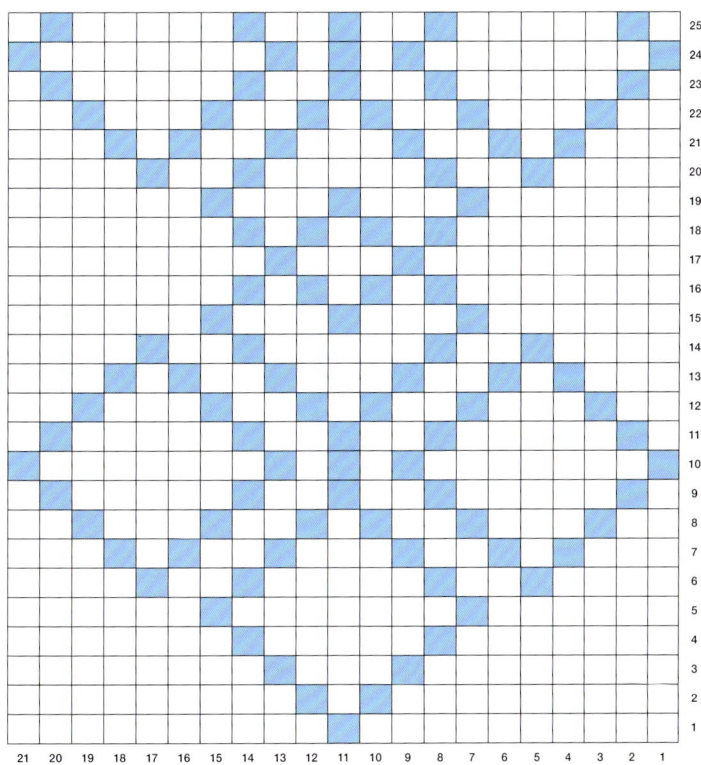

COLORWORK CHART B

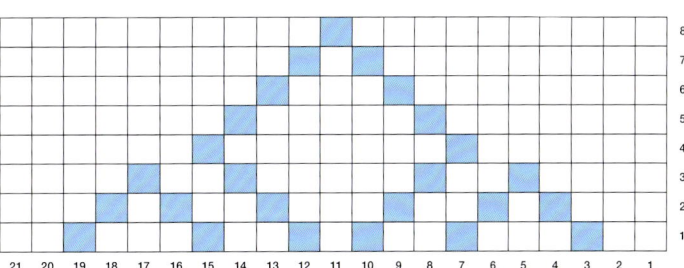

Matis

SIZES
W5½/6 (W7/8, W9/9½ [M7/7½], W11/12 [M8½/9], M10/11)

MATERIALS
Lana Grossa Meilenweit 100 Merino Extrafine: 75% Merino wool, 25% polyamide/nylon; 459 yd (420 m) per 3.5 oz (100 g)

- Blue-Green 2410: 1 skein
- Lilac 2421: 1 skein

Lana Grossa Cool Wool 4 Socks: 75% Merino extrafine wool, 25% polyamide/nylon; 459 yd (420 m) per 3.5 oz (100 g)

- Jeans Blue 7704: 1 skein
- Bordeaux 7716: 1 skein

Lana Grossa Meilenweit 100: 80% wool, 20% polyamide/nylon; 459 yd (420 m) per 3.5 oz (100 g)

- Orange 1384: 1 skein

DPN set in US size 2 (2.5–3.0 mm) (or other preferred needle type, see page 10)

Stitch markers

Tapestry needle

Scissors

GAUGE
In stockinette stitch with US size 2 needles (2.5–3.0 mm):

28 sts and 40 rows = 4 x 4 in (10 x 10 cm)

BASIC PATTERN
STOCKINETTE STITCH

In rows: Knit on RS, purl on WS.
In rounds: Knit all stitches in all rounds.

CUFF RIBBING

2x2 ribbing: *Knit 2, purl 2*, repeat from * to * continuously.

CONSTRUCTION
The sock is worked from the cuff down, featuring a turned heel and paired banded toe decreases. The colorwork pattern is worked all around the leg, and a stripe pattern is worked all around the foot.

INSTRUCTIONS
CUFF

CO 60 (60/64/64/68) sts in Blue-Green, distribute sts evenly onto 4 DPNs [= 15 (15/16/16/17) sts per needle], and join to work in the round.

Work 15 rounds [= about 1.5 in (3.5 cm)] in cuff ribbing.

LEG

Change color to Lilac.

Rounds 1–7: Knit all stitches.

Change color to Jeans Blue.

Rounds 8–9: Knit all stitches.

Change color to Lilac.

Rounds 10–12: Knit all stitches.

LEFT SOCK
SIZES W5½/6, W7/8

In these sizes, the alternating color change between Bordeaux and Orange does not quite fit the stitch count in the round. When working these sizes, you might want to shift the pattern so the spot with repetitive color ends up on the interior side of the leg.

Rounds 13–31: Knit 2, work sts 10–25 of the colorwork chart twice [= 32 sts], work sts 10–16 of the colorwork chart [= 7 sts], work sts 9–17 of the colorwork chart [9 sts], work sts 2–9 of the colorwork chart [= 8 sts], knit 2 [= total of 60 sts].

SIZES W9/9½ [M7/7½], W11/12 [M8½/9]

Rounds 13–31: Work sts 10–25 of the colorwork chart four times in all.

SIZE M10/11

Rounds 13–31: Knit 2, work sts 10–25 of the colorwork chart four times in all, knit 2.

RIGHT SOCK
SIZES W5½/6, W7/8

In these sizes, the alternating color change between Bordeaux and Orange does not quite fit the stitch count in the round. When working these sizes, you might want to shift the pattern so the spot with repetitive color ends up on the interior side of the leg.

Rounds 13–31: Knit 2, work sts 2–17 of the colorwork chart [= 16 sts], work sts 2–9 of the colorwork chart [= 8 sts], work sts 10–25 of the colorwork chart twice [= 32 sts], knit 2 [= total of 60 sts].

SIZES W9/9½ [M7/7½], W11/12 [M8½/9]

Rounds 13–31: Work sts 10–25 of the colorwork chart four times in all.

SIZE M10/11

Rounds 13–31: Knit 2, work sts 10–25 of the colorwork chart four times in all, knit 2.

Rounds 32–34: Knit all stitches.

Change color to Jeans Blue.

Rounds 35–36: Knit all stitches.

Change color to Lilac.

Rounds 37–42: Knit all stitches.

Round 43: Knit all sts on needles 1, 2, and 3.

Change color to Blue-Green, then knit all sts on needle 4.

HEEL AND FOOT

Work the turned heel in stockinette stitch over the 30 (30/32/32/34) sts of needles 4 and 1 according to Basic instructions (see page 37). Begin with Blue-Green.

Work the pick-up and gusset in Lilac until a total of 10 rounds (including the leg rounds) have been worked in Lilac.

After this, continuously alternate working 2 rounds in Jeans Blue and 7 rounds in Lilac.

TOE DECREASES

After having worked 6.25 (7/8/8/8.5) in [16 (17.5/20.5/20.5/22) cm] (measured from the middle of the heel), change color to Blue-Green, and begin working paired banded toe decreases (see page 40).

FINISHING

Weave in all ends.

COLORWORK CHART

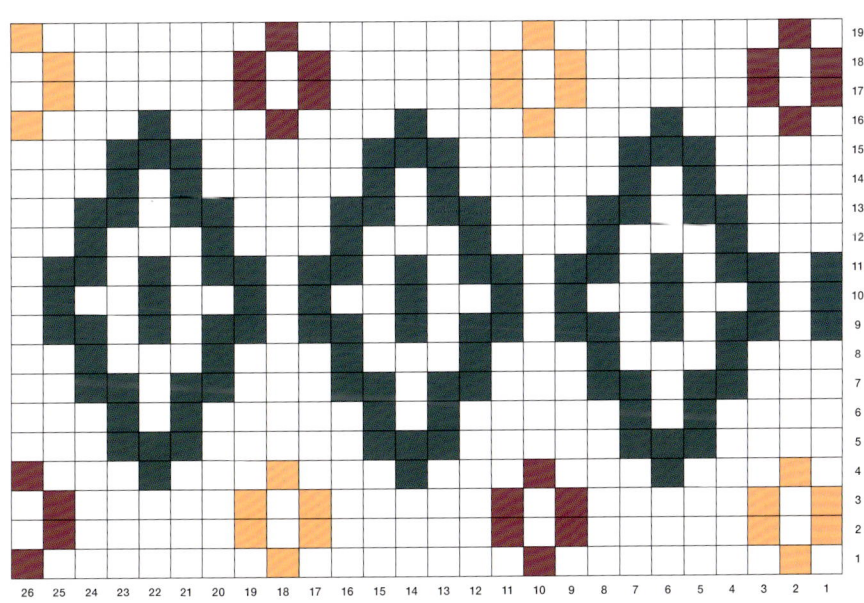

Pinja

SIZES
W5½/6 (W7/8, W9/9½ [M7/7½], W11/12 [M8½/9], M10/11)

MATERIALS
Lana Grossa Cool Wool 4 Socks: 75% Merino extrafine wool, 25% polyamide/nylon; 459 yd (420 m) per 3.5 oz (100 g)

- Light Gray 7709: 1 skein

Lana Grossa Meilenweit 100 Merino Extrafine: 75% Merino wool, 25% polyamide/nylon; 459 yd (420 m) per 3.5 oz (100 g)

- Lilac 2435: 1 skein

Lana Grossa Meilenweit 100: 80% wool, 20% polyamide/nylon; 459 yd (420 m) per 3.5 oz (100 g)

- Olive Green 1369: 1 skein

DPN set in US size 2 (2.5–3.0 mm) (or other preferred needle type, see page 10)

Stitch markers

Tapestry needle

Scissors

GAUGE
In stockinette stitch with US size 2 needles (2.5–3.0 mm):

28 sts and 40 rows = 4 x 4 in (10 x 10 cm)

BASIC PATTERN
STOCKINETTE STITCH
In rows: Knit on RS, purl on WS.
In rounds: Knit all stitches in all rounds.

CUFF RIBBING
2x3 ribbing: *Knit 2, purl 3*, repeat from * to * continuously.

CONSTRUCTION
The sock is worked from the toe up to the cuff and features a boomerang heel. The colorwork pattern on the top of the foot is worked with two strands of yarn held together. At the end, a long fold-over cuff in a ribbing pattern is worked.

INSTRUCTIONS

TOE SECTION

For the toe section, using Light Gray and the long-tail cast-on for toe-up socks (see page 42), CO 8 sts.

Work increases until you have a total of 60 (60/64/64/68) sts on the needles [= 15 (15/16/16/17) sts per needle].

FOOT

Work stockinette stitch in the round over all sts until piece has reached a length of approx. 3 (3.25/3.75/4/4.25) in [8 (8.5/9.5/10/11) cm] (measured from toe section), in the next round, k18 (18/20/20/22), pm, k23, pm, k19 (19/21/21/23).

In the next 25 rounds, work the colorwork pattern (Colorwork Chart A for the left foot/Colorwork Chart B for the right foot) over the 23 sts between the markers with two strands each in Lilac and Olive Green, respectively, held together.

After having completed Round 25 of the colorwork chart, remove the markers, then work all stitches in stockinette stitch.

HEEL

After having worked 6.25 (7/7.5/8/8.75) in [16 (17.5/19/20.5/22) cm] (measured from tip of toe), begin working a boomerang heel in stockinette stitch according to Basic instructions (see page 36) over the 30 (30/32/32/34) sts of needles 4 and 1.

LEG AND CUFF

After having completed the boomerang heel, work 25 rnds in stockinette stitch.

SIZES W9/9½ [M7/7½], W11/12 [M8½/9]

In the last round before the cuff, at the beginning of the round, increase 1 stitch [= 65 sts].

SIZE M10/11

In the last round before the cuff, increase 2 sts, evenly spaced [= 70 sts].

For the cuff, work in 2x3 ribbing as follows: *Knit 2, purl 3*, repeat from * to * continuously until the cuff measures 5 in (12.5 cm). Bind off all stitches loosely in pattern (knitting the knit stitches and purling the purl stitches), making sure the opening does not turn out too tight.

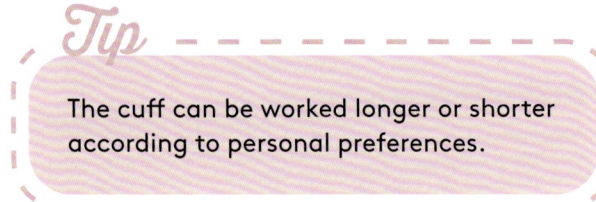

Tip: The cuff can be worked longer or shorter according to personal preferences.

FINISHING

Weave in all ends, and fold the cuff over twice.

COLORWORK CHART A (LEFT FOOT)

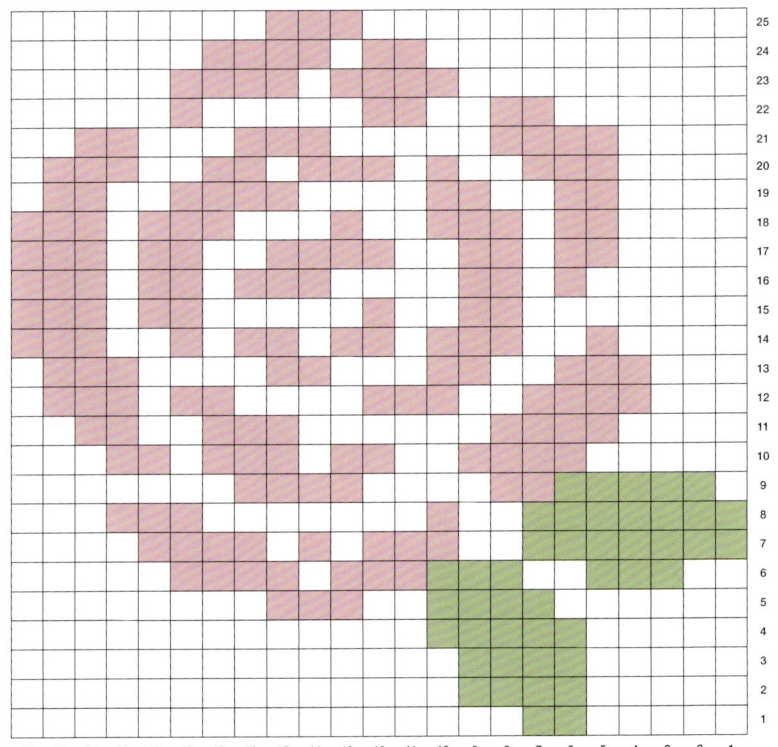

COLORWORK CHART B (RIGHT FOOT)

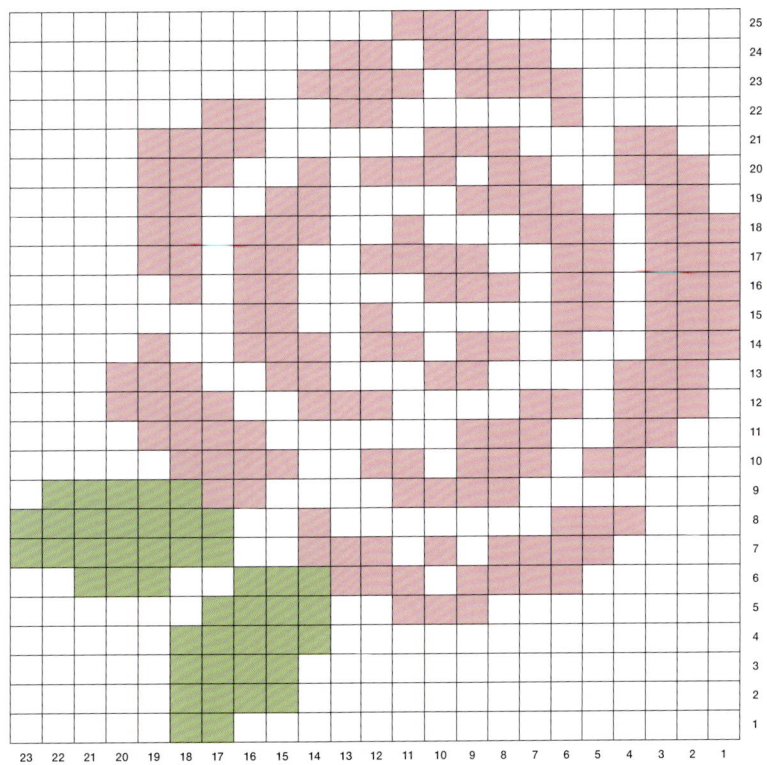

Kuldar

SIZES
W5½/6 (W7/8, W9/9½ [M7/7½], W11/12 [M8½/9], M10/11)

MATERIALS
Lana Grossa Meilenweit 100 Seta: 55% Merino wool, 25% polyamide/nylon, 20% silk; 437 yd (400 m) per 3.5 oz (100 g)

- Reseda Green 29: 1 skein
- Raspberry Red 33: 1 skein

Lana Grossa Cool Wool 4 Socks: 75% Merino wool, 25% polyamide/nylon; 459 yd (420 m) per 3.5 oz (100 g)

- Dark Green 7701: 1 skein

DPN set in US size 2 (2.5–3.0 mm) (or other preferred needle type, see page 10)

Stitch markers

Tapestry needle

Scissors

GAUGE
In stockinette stitch with US size 2 needles (2.5–3.0 mm):

30 sts and 42 rows = 4 x 4 in (10 x 10 cm)

BASIC PATTERN
STOCKINETTE STITCH
In rows: Knit on RS, purl on WS.
In rounds: Knit all stitches in all rounds.

CUFF RIBBING
1x1 twisted ribbing: *Knit 1 through the back loop, purl 1*, repeat from * to * continuously.

CONSTRUCTION
The sneaker sock is worked from the cuff down, starting with a rolled edge, and features a boomerang heel and paired banded toe decreases. The colorwork pattern is worked on the top of the foot.

INSTRUCTIONS

CUFF

CO 60 (60/64/64/68) sts in Raspberry Red, distribute sts evenly onto 4 DPNs [= 15 (15/16/16/17) sts per needle], and join to work in the round.

Round 1: Knit all stitches.

Change color to Reseda Green.

Rounds 2–5: Knit all stitches.

Rounds 6–10: *Knit 1 through the back loop, purl 1*, repeat from * to * continuously.

Rounds 11–15: Knit all stitches.

HEEL

Work a boomerang heel in stockinette stitch in Reseda Green over the 30 (30/32/32/34) sts of needles 4 and 1 according to Basic instructions (see page 36).

FOOT

Work stockinette stitch in the round over all sts until the piece has reached a length of approx. 3 (3.25/3.75/4/4.25) in [8 (8.5/9.5/10/11) cm] (measured from the middle of the heel), then in the next round, k20 (20/22/22/24), pm, k21, pm, k19 (19/21/21/23).

In the next 21 rounds, work the colorwork pattern with two strands each in Dark Green and Raspberry Red, respectively, held together over the 21 sts between the markers.

After having completed Round 21 of the colorwork chart, remove the markers, and work all stitches in stockinette stitch.

TOE DECREASES

After having worked approx. 6.25 (7/7.5/8/8.75) in [16 (17.5/19/20.5/22) cm] (measured from the middle of the heel), work one round in Raspberry Red, then work paired banded toe decreases according to Basic instructions (see page 40) in Reseda Green.

FINISHING

Weave in all ends.

COLORWORK CHART

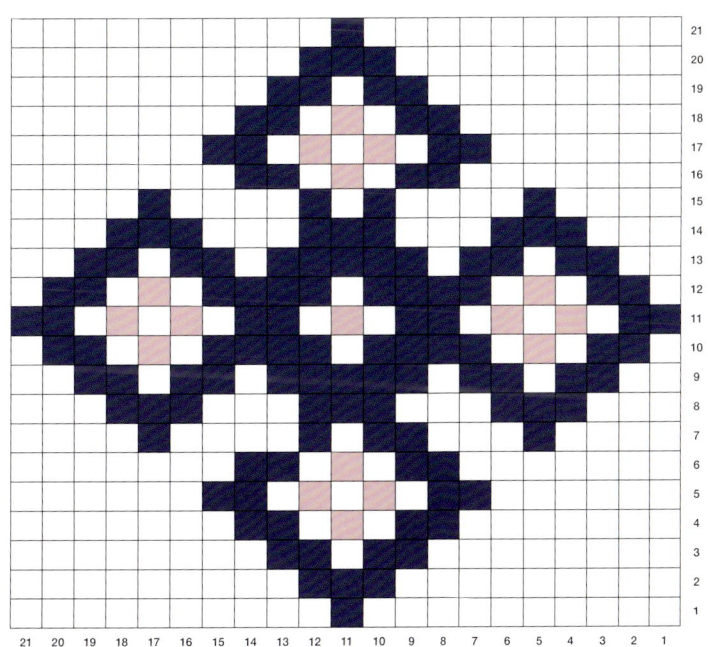

Kuldar 71

72 Projects

Sirja

SIZES
W5½/6 (W7/8, W9/9½ [M7/7½], W11/12 [M8½/9], M10/11)

MATERIALS
Lana Grossa Cool Wool 4 Socks: 75% Merino wool, 25% polyamide/nylon; 459 yd (420 m) per 3.5 oz (100 g)

- Night Blue 7705: 1 skein

Lana Grossa Meilenweit 100: 80% wool, 20% polyamide/nylon; 459 yd (420 m) per 3.5 oz (100 g)

- Orange 1384: 1 skein

DPN set in US size 2 (2.5–3.0 mm) (or other preferred needle type, see page 10)

Stitch markers

Tapestry needle

Scissors

GAUGE
In stockinette stitch with US size 2 needles (2.5–3.0 mm):

28 sts and 40 rows = 4 x 4 in (10 x 10 cm)

BASIC PATTERN
STOCKINETTE STITCH
In rows: Knit on RS, purl on WS.
In rounds: Knit all stitches in all rounds.

CUFF RIBBING
2x2 ribbing: *Knit 2, purl 2*, repeat from * to * continuously.

CONSTRUCTION
The sock is worked from the cuff down, featuring a boomerang heel and paired banded toe decreases. The colorwork pattern on the leg is worked with two strands of yarn held together.

INSTRUCTIONS

CUFF

CO 60 (60/64/64/68) sts in Night Blue, distribute sts evenly onto 4 DPNs [= 15 (15/16/16/17) sts per needle], and join to work in the round.

Work 12 rounds [= 1.25 in (3 cm)] in cuff ribbing.

LEG AND HEEL

Work 9 rounds in stockinette stitch.

In Round 10, k23 (23/25/25/27), pm, k15, pm, k22 (22/24/24/26).

Work 65 (65/73/73/81) rounds in stockinette stitch, working the colorwork pattern with two strands of Orange held together according to the colorwork rounds listed below, over the 15 sts between the markers. When piece has reached a length of approx. 5.75 in (14.5 cm) (measured from cast-on edge), begin working a boomerang heel over the 30 (30/32/32/34) sts of needles 4 and 1 according to Basic instructions (see page 36), continuing the pattern motif on the front of the sock in intermittent rounds.

SIZES W5½/6, W7/8

Rounds 1–8: Work Rounds 1–8 of the colorwork chart.

Rounds 9–56: Work Rounds 9–24 of the colorwork chart three times in all.

Rounds 57–65: Work Rounds 17–25 of the colorwork chart.

SIZES W9/9½ [M7/7½], W11/12 [M8½/9]

Rounds 1–8: Work Rounds 1–8 of the colorwork chart.

Rounds 9–56: Work Rounds 9–24 of the colorwork chart three times in all.

Rounds 57–73: Work Rounds 9–25 of the colorwork chart.

SIZE M10/11

Rounds 1–8: Work Rounds 1–8 of the colorwork chart.

Rounds 9–72: Work Rounds 9–24 of the colorwork chart four times in all.

Rounds 73–81: Work Rounds 17–25 of the colorwork chart.

FOOT AND PAIRED BANDED TOE DECREASES

Work in stockinette stitch, completing all 65 (65/73/73/81) rounds of the pattern motif. After this, continue in stockinette stitch until the foot (measured from the middle of the heel) measures 6.25 (7/7.5/8/8.75) in [16 (17.5/19/20.5/22) cm]. Finish by working paired banded toe decreases according to Basic instructions (see page 40).

FINISHING

Weave in all ends.

COLORWORK CHART

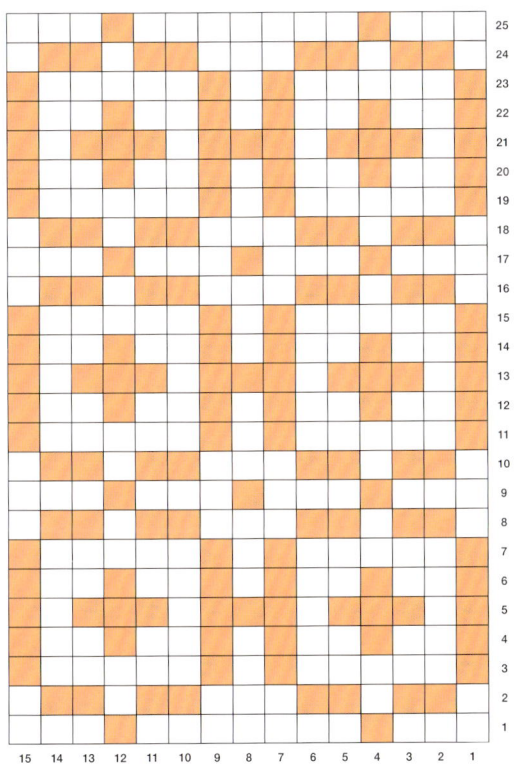

Ivar

SIZES
W5½/6 (W7/8, W9/9½ [M7/7½], W11/12 [M8½/9], M10/11)

MATERIALS
Lana Grossa Meilenweit 100 Tweed: 80% wool, 20% polyamide/nylon; 459 yd (420 m) per 3.5 oz (100 g)
- Gray Blue 171: 1 skein

Lana Grossa Cool Wool 4 Socks: 75% Merino wool, 25% polyamide/nylon; 459 yd (420 m) per 3.5 oz (100 g)
- Golden Yellow 7713: 1 skein
- Turquoise 7703: 1 skein

DPN set in US size 2 (2.5–3.0 mm) (or other preferred needle type, see page 10)

Stitch markers

Tapestry needle

Scissors

GAUGE
In stockinette stitch with US size 2 needles (2.5–3.0 mm):
28 sts and 40 rows = 4 x 4 in (10 x 10 cm)

BASIC PATTERN
STOCKINETTE STITCH
In rows: Knit on RS, purl on WS.
In rounds: Knit all stitches in all rounds.

CUFF RIBBING
2x2 ribbing: *Knit 2, purl 2*, repeat from * to * continuously.

CONSTRUCTION
The sock is worked from the cuff down and features a boomerang heel and paired banded toe decreases. The colorwork pattern is worked on the leg with two strands of yarn held together.

INSTRUCTIONS

CUFF
CO 60 (60/64/64/68) sts in Gray Blue, distribute sts evenly onto 4 DPNs [= 15 (15/16/16/17) sts per needle], and join to work in the round.

Work 15 rounds [= 1.5 in (3.5 cm)] in cuff ribbing.

LEG
Knit one round.

LEFT SOCK
K33 (33/35/35/37), pm, k8, pm, k19 (19/21/21/23).

RIGHT SOCK
K19 (19/21/21/23), pm, k8, pm, k33 (33/35/35/37).

Work 43 rounds in stockinette stitch, at the same time working the colorwork pattern over the 8 sts between the markers with two strands each held together in Golden Yellow and Turquoise, respectively, as follows:

Rounds 1–31: Work Rounds 1–31 of the colorwork chart.

Rounds 32–43: Work Rounds 20–31 of the colorwork chart.

Remove the markers, and work 10 rounds in stockinette stitch.

HEEL
Work a boomerang heel according to Basic instructions (see page 36) in stockinette stitch over the 30 (30/32/32/34) sts of needles 4 and 1.

FOOT AND TOE DECREASES
Work stockinette stitch in the round until the foot (measured from the middle of the heel) measures 6.25 (7/7.5/8/8.75) in [16 (17.5/19/20.5/22) cm]. Finish by working paired banded toe decreases according to Basic instructions (see page 40).

FINISHING
Weave in all ends.

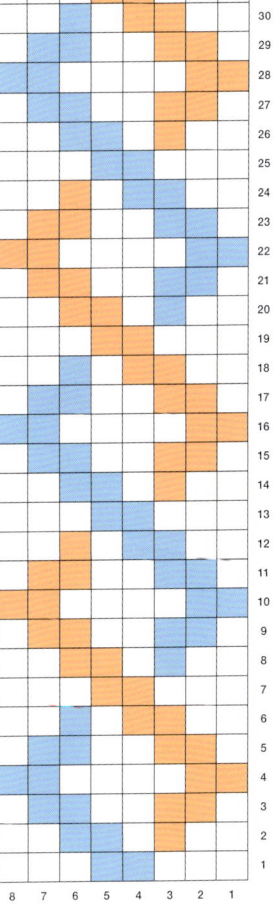

COLORWORK CHART

Ivar 79

Ilme

SIZES
W5½/6 (W7/8, W9/9½ [M7/7½], W11/12 [M8½/9], M10/11)

MATERIALS
Lana Grossa Meilenweit 100 Merino Extrafine: 75% Merino wool, 25% polyamide/nylon; 459 yd (420 m) per 3.5 oz (100 g)
- Jade 2440: 1 skein

Lana Grossa Meilenweit 100: 80% wool, 20% polyamide/nylon; 459 yd (420 m) per 3.5 oz (100 g)
- Blue 1342: 1 skein

Lana Grossa Cool Wool 4 Socks: 75% Merino wool, 25% polyamide/nylon; 459 yd (420 m) per 3.5 oz (100 g)
- Golden Yellow 7713: 1 skein

DPN set in US size 2 (2.5–3.0 mm) (or other preferred needle type, see page 10)

Stitch markers

Tapestry needle

Scissors

GAUGE
In stockinette stitch with US size 2 needles (2.5–3.0 mm):
28 sts and 40 rows = 4 x 4 in (10 x 10 cm)

BASIC PATTERN
STOCKINETTE STITCH
In rows: Knit on RS, purl on WS.
In rounds: Knit all stitches in all rounds.

CUFF RIBBING
1x1 twisted ribbing: *Knit 1 through the back loop, purl 1*, repeat from * to * continuously.

CONSTRUCTION
The sock is worked from the cuff down, featuring a boomerang heel and paired banded toe decreases. The colorwork pattern on the leg is worked with two strands of yarn held together.

INSTRUCTIONS

CUFF

CO 60 (60/64/64/68) sts in Jade, distribute sts evenly onto 4 DPNs [= 15 (15/16/16/17) sts per needle], and join to work in the round.

Work 15 rounds [= 1.5 in (3.5 cm)] in cuff ribbing.

LEG

Knit one round.

Change color to Blue.

Knit 2 rounds.

In Round 4, k3, pm, k15, pm, k5 (5/7/7/7), pm, k15, pm, k5 (5/6/6/8), pm, k15, pm, k2 (2/3/3/5).

Work 19 rounds in stockinette stitch, at the same time working the colorwork pattern with two strands each held together in Golden Yellow and Jade over the 15 sts between the markers.

Knit two rounds, removing markers as you encounter them.

Change color to Jade.

Knit 3 rounds.

Change color to Blue.

Knit one round.

In the next round, k8, pm, k5 (5/7/7/8), pm, k15, pm, k5 (5/6/6/7), pm, k15, pm, k5 (5/6/6/8), pm, k7.

Work 19 rounds in stockinette stitch, at the same time working the colorwork pattern with two strands each held together in Golden Yellow and Jade over the 15 sts between the markers.

Knit three rounds, removing markers as you encounter them.

Change color to Jade.

Knit 3 rounds.

HEEL

Work a boomerang heel in stockinette stitch in Jade over the 30 (30/32/32/34) sts of needles 4 and 1 according to Basic instructions (see page 36).

FOOT AND TOE DECREASES

Work stockinette stitch in the round until the foot (measured from the middle of the heel) measures 6.25 (7/7.5/8/8.75) in [16 (17.5/19/20.5/22) cm]. Finish by working paired banded toe decreases according to Basic instructions (see page 40).

FINISHING

Weave in all ends.

COLORWORK CHART

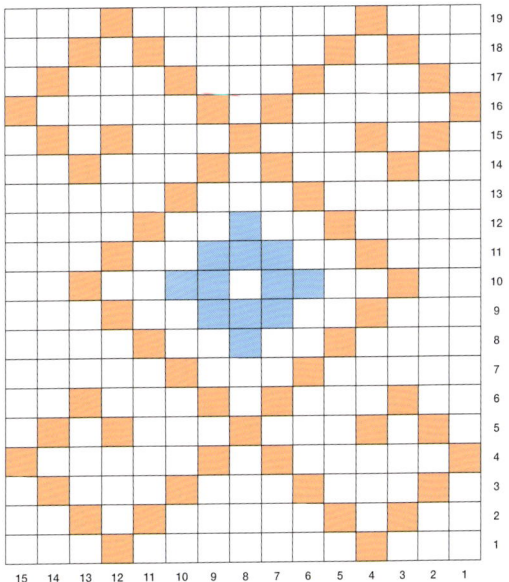

Ilme 83

Reelika

SIZES
W5½/6 (W7/8, W9/9½ [M7/7½], W11/12 [M8½/9], M10/11)

MATERIALS
Lana Grossa Meilenweit 50 Cashmere: 70% wool, 25% polyamide/nylon, 5% cashmere; 230 yd (210 m) per 1.8 oz (50 g)
- Bordeaux 44: 2 skeins
- Gray 13: 1 skein
- Tulip Green 53: 1 skein

DPN set in US size 2 (2.5–3.0 mm) (or other preferred needle type, see page 10)

Stitch markers

Tapestry needle

Scissors

GAUGE
In stockinette stitch with US size 2 needles (2.5–3.0 mm):
30 sts and 40 rows = 4 x 4 in (10 x 10 cm)

BASIC PATTERN
STOCKINETTE STITCH
In rows: Knit on RS, purl on WS.
In rounds: Knit all stitches in all rounds.

CUFF RIBBING
2x2 ribbing: *Knit 2, purl 2*, repeat from * to * continuously.

CONSTRUCTION
The sock is worked from the cuff down, featuring a classic turned heel and paired banded toe decreases. The colorwork pattern is worked with yarn held single all over the front of the sock.

INSTRUCTIONS

CUFF

CO 60 (60/64/64/68) sts in Bordeaux, distribute sts evenly onto 4 DPNs [= 15 (15/16/16/17) sts per needle], and join to work in the round.

Work 15 rounds in cuff ribbing pattern [= 1.5 in (3.5 cm)].

LEG

Change color to Gray, k16 (16/18/18/20), pm, k29, pm, k15 (15/17/17/19).

> **Tip**
> To prevent the marker from sliding off the needles, stitches may be moved to adjoining needles where required.

In Gray, work 50 rounds in stockinette stitch, at the same time working the colorwork pattern with one strand each in Bordeaux and Tulip Green, respectively, over the 29 sts between the markers. Repeat Rounds 1–16 of the colorwork chart continuously, at the same time changing between Bordeaux and Tulip Green as desired.

HEEL

In Bordeaux, work a turned heel according to Basic instructions (see page 37) over the 30 (30/32/32/34) sts of needles 4 and 1. For picking up gusset stitches and working the gusset, change color to Gray, at the same time continuing the colorwork pattern on the front of the sock in all rounds.

PLEASE NOTE: If you had previously distributed your stitches on the needles a different way than listed, you will need to rearrange them in the original way in order to work the turned heel.

FOOT

Continue the colorwork pattern over the foot until 6 (7/7.25/8/8.5) in [15.5 (17.5/18.5/20/21.5) cm] (measured from the middle of the heel) have been worked.

Work 2 more rounds in Gray without colorwork. Remove the markers, and if applicable, redistribute the stitches in the original way before starting the toe decreases.

TOE DECREASES

Change color to Bordeaux and work paired banded toe decreases according to Basic instructions (see page 40).

FINISHING

Weave in all ends.

COLORWORK CHART

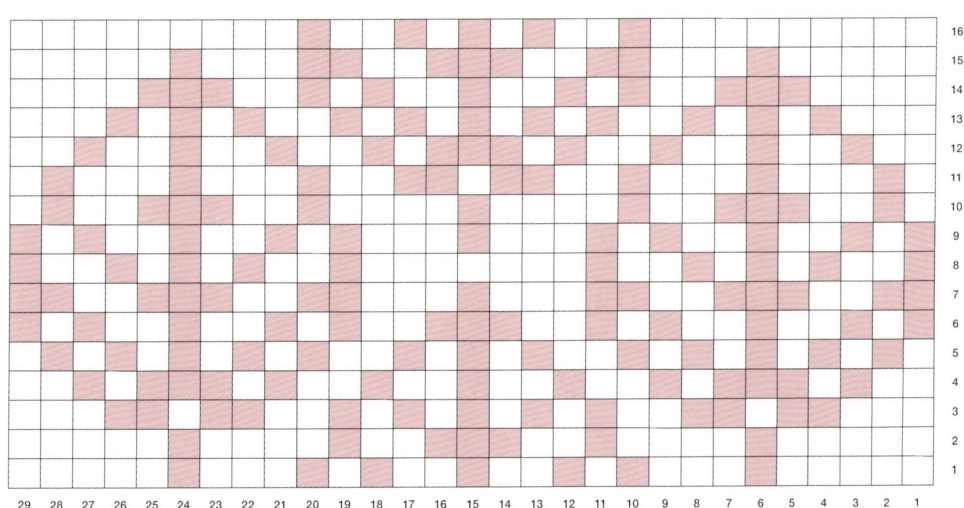

Veiko

SIZES
W5½/6 (W7/8, W9/9½ [M7/7½], W11/12 [M8½/9], M10/11)

MATERIALS
Lana Grossa Meilenweit 100: 80% wool, 20% polyamide/nylon; 459 yd (420 m) per 3.5 oz (100 g)

- Heather Grey 1103: 1 skein
- Heather Brown 1334: 1 skein

DPN set in US size 2 (2.5–3.0 mm) (or other preferred needle type, see page 10)

Stitch markers

Tapestry needle

Scissors

GAUGE
In stockinette stitch with US size 2 needles (2.5–3.0 mm):

28 sts and 40 rows = 4 x 4 in (10 x 10 cm)

BASIC PATTERN
STOCKINETTE STITCH
In rows: Knit on RS, purl on WS.
In rounds: Knit all stitches in all rounds.

CUFF RIBBING
2x2 ribbing: *Knit 2, purl 2*, repeat from * to * continuously.

CONSTRUCTION
The sock is worked in two colors from the cuff down, featuring a boomerang heel and paired banded toe decreases. The colorwork pattern on the leg is worked with two strands of yarn held together.

INSTRUCTIONS

CUFF

CO 60 (60/64/64/68) sts in Heather Grey, distribute sts evenly onto 4 DPNs [= 15 (15/16/16/17) sts per needle], and join to work in the round.

Work 12 rounds [= 1.25 in (3 cm)] in cuff ribbing.

LEG

Work 14 rounds in stockinette stitch.

In the next round, k22 (22/24/24/26), pm, k16, pm, k22 (22/24/24/26).

In the next 13 rounds, work the colorwork pattern in Heather Brown over the 16 sts between the markers.

Change main color to Heather Brown, and continue the colorwork pattern in Heather Grey in Rounds 14 through 32.

When all rounds of the colorwork pattern have been completed, remove the two markers, and work one round more in Heather Brown in stockinette stitch.

HEEL

Work a boomerang heel in stockinette stitch in Heather Brown over the 30 (30/32/32/34) sts of needles 4 and 1 according to Basic instructions (see page 36).

FOOT AND TOE DECREASES

Work stockinette stitch in the round until the foot (measured from the middle of the heel) measures 6.25 (7/7.5/8/8.75) in [16 (17.5/19/20.5/22) cm]. Finish by working paired banded toe decreases according to Basic instructions (see page 40).

FINISHING

Weave in all ends.

COLORWORK CHART

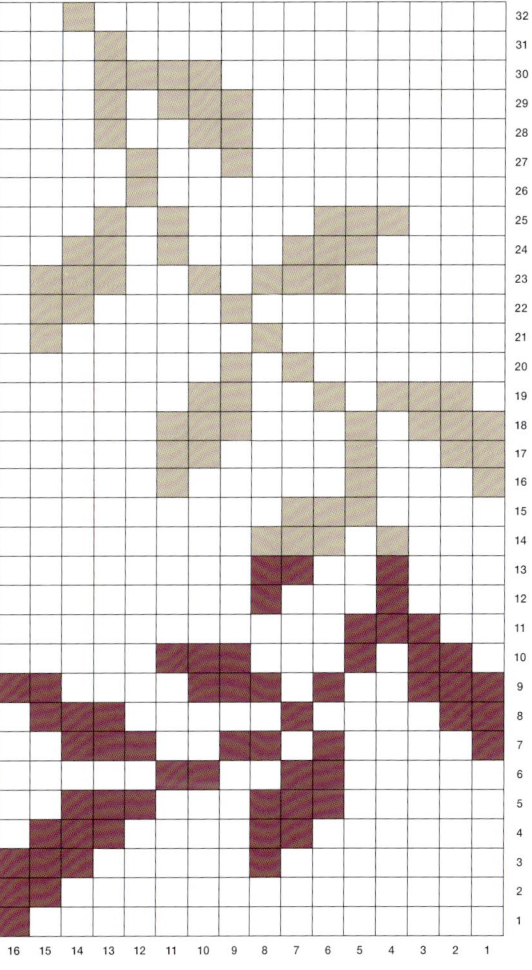

Kalev

SIZES
W5½/6 (W7/8, W9/9½ [M7/7½], W11/12 [M8½/9], M10/11)

MATERIALS
Lana Grossa Cool Wool 4 Socks: 75% Merino wool, 25% polyamide/nylon; 459 yd (420 m) per 3.5 oz (100 g)
- Bordeaux 7716: 1 skein
- Dark Green 7701: 1 skein

Lana Grossa Meilenweit 100 Seta: 55% wool, 25% polyamide/nylon, 20% silk; 437 yd (400 m) per 3.5 oz (100 g)
- Blackberry 26: 1 skein
- Clay Brown 32: 1 skein

DPN set in size US 2 (2.5–3.0 mm) (or other preferred needle type, see page 10)

Stitch markers

Tapestry needle

Scissors

GAUGE
In stockinette stitch with US size 2 needles (2.5–3.0 mm):
28 sts and 40 rows = 4 x 4 in (10 x 10 cm)

BASIC PATTERN
STOCKINETTE STITCH
In rows: Knit on RS, purl on WS.
In rounds: Knit all stitches in all rounds.

CUFF RIBBING
1x1 twisted ribbing: *Knit 1 through the back loop, purl 1*, repeat from * to * continuously.

CONSTRUCTION
The sock is worked from the cuff down, featuring a classic turned heel and paired banded toe decreases. The colorwork pattern at the side of the leg is worked with two strands of yarn held together.

INSTRUCTIONS

CUFF

CO 60 (60/64/64/68) sts in Bordeaux, distribute sts evenly onto 4 DPNs [= 15 (15/16/16/17) sts per needle], and join to work in the round.

Work 15 rounds [= 1.5 in (3.5 cm)] in cuff ribbing.

LEG

Change color to Blackberry, and work 3 rounds in stockinette stitch.

LEFT SOCK

In Round 4, k2 (2/4/4/6), pm, k27, pm, k31 (31/33/33/35).

RIGHT SOCK

In Round 4, k31 (31/33/33/35), pm, k27, pm, k2 (2/4/4/6).

Work 39 rounds in Blackberry in stockinette stitch, at the same time working the colorwork pattern over the 27 sts between the markers with two strands each held together in colors Dark Green, Bordeaux, and Clay Brown, respectively.

Remove the markers, then work 5 rounds in stockinette stitch in Blackberry.

HEEL

Change color to Dark Green, and work a turned heel over the 30 (30/32/32/34) sts of needles 4 and 1 according to Basic instructions (see page 37).

For picking up gusset stitches and working the gusset, change color to Blackberry.

FOOT

Work stockinette stitch in the round until the foot (measured from the middle of the heel) measures 6.25 (7/7.5/8/8.75) in [16 (17.5/19/20.5/22) cm].

TOE DECREASES

Change color to Bordeaux, and work paired banded toe decreases according to Basic instructions (see page 40).

FINISHING

Weave in all ends.

COLORWORK CHART

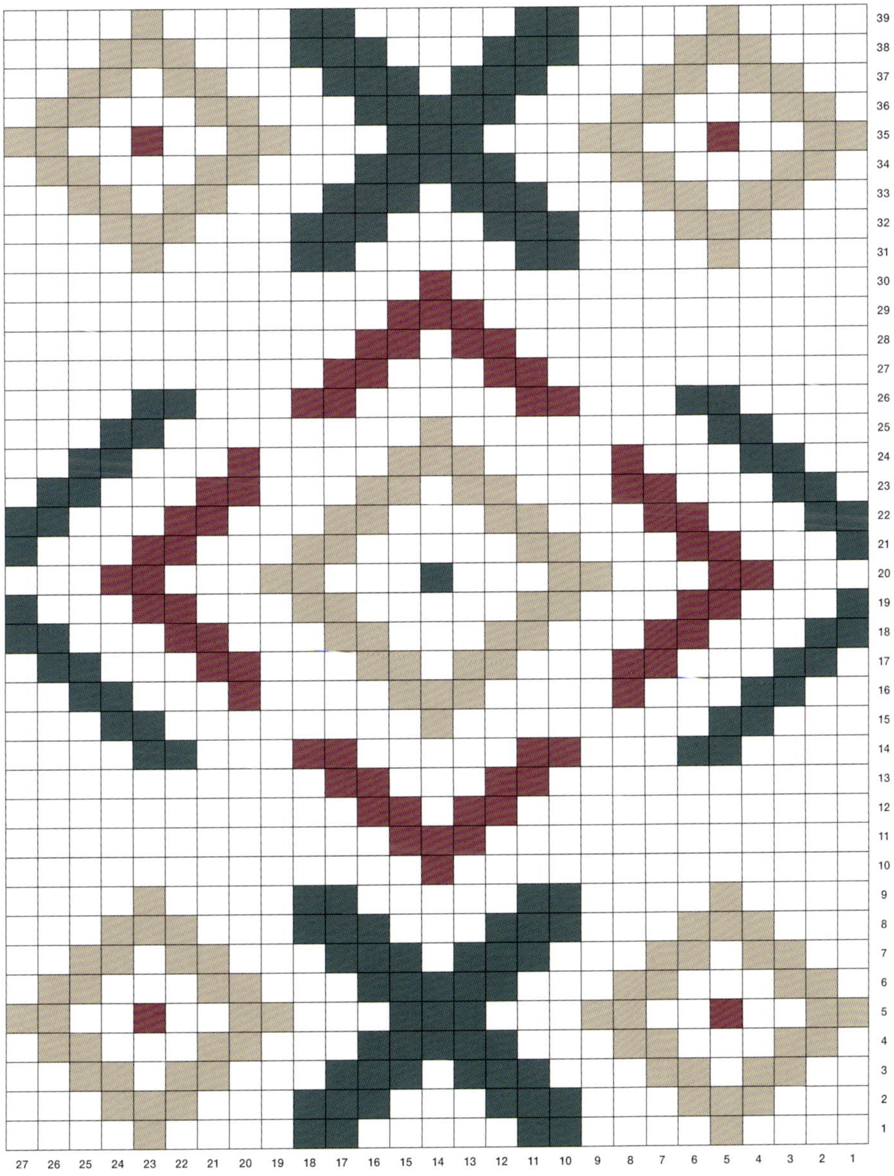

Kalev 95

Kaisa

SIZES

W5½/6 (W7/8, W9/9½ [M7/7½], W11/12 [M8½/9], M10/11)

MATERIALS

Lana Grossa Cool Wool 4 Socks: 75% wool, 25% polyamide/nylon; 459 yd (420 m) per 3.5 oz (100 g)

- Raw White 7710: 1 skein
- Beige 7711: 1 skein
- Rust Brown 7712: 1 skein

Lana Grossa Meilenweit 100 Seta: 55% wool, 25% polyamide/nylon, 20% silk; 437 yd (400 m) per 3.5 oz (100 g)

- Clay Red 27: 1 skein

DPN set in US size 2 (2.5–3.0 mm) (or other preferred needle type, see page 10)

Stitch markers

Tapestry needle

Scissors

GAUGE

In stockinette stitch with US size 2 needles (2.5–3.0 mm):

28 sts and 40 rows = 4 x 4 in (10 x 10 cm)

BASIC PATTERN

STOCKINETTE STITCH

In rows: Knit on RS, purl on WS.
In rounds: Knit all stitches in all rounds.

CONSTRUCTION

The sock is worked from the cuff down with a wide cuff featuring picots, a boomerang heel, and paired banded toe decreases. The colorwork pattern on the front of the sock is worked in the wide colorblock sections with two strands of yarn held together.

INSTRUCTIONS
CUFF
CO 60 (60/64/64/68) sts in Raw White, distribute sts evenly onto 4 DPNs [= 15 (15/16/16/17) sts per needle], and join to work in the round.

Work 10 rounds [= 1.5 in (3.5 cm)] in stockinette stitch.

For the picot edge, work one round as follows:

K2tog, 1 yo, repeat from * to * continuously.

In the next round, knit all stitches and all yarn overs.

Work 10 rounds in stockinette stitch.

Fold the cast-on edge over to the inside of the sock, and knit stitches together in pairs to the end of the round (always knitting 1 st of the current round together with 1 st of the CO round).

LEG
K20 (20/22/22/24), pm, k21, pm, k19 (19/21/21/23).

Change color to Beige.

Knit 5 rounds.

In the next 5 rounds, work Colorwork Chart A in Raw White and Clay Red over the 21 sts between the markers.

Knit 5 rounds.

Change color to Raw White.

Knit 3 rounds.

Change color to Clay Red.

Knit 5 rounds.

In the next 5 rounds, work Colorwork Chart B in Raw White over the 21 sts between the markers.

Knit 5 rounds.

Change color to Raw White.

Knit 3 rounds.

Change color to Rust Brown.

Knit 5 rounds.

In the next 5 rounds, work Colorwork Chart A in Raw White and Clay Red over the 21 sts between the markers.

Knit 5 rounds.

Change color to Raw White.

Knit one round.

HEEL
Work a boomerang heel according to Basic instructions (see page 36) in Raw White in stockinette stitch over the 30 (30/32/32/34) sts of needles 4 and 1.

FOOT
Change color to Beige.

Knit 5 rounds.

In the next 5 rounds, work Colorwork Chart B in Raw White over the 21 sts between the markers.

Knit 5 rounds.

Change color to Raw White.

Knit 3 rounds.

Change color to Clay Red.

Knit 5 rounds.

In the next 5 rounds, work Colorwork Chart A in Raw White and Rust Brown over the 21 sts between the markers.

Knit 5 rounds.

Change color to Raw White.

Knit 3 rounds.

Continue the color sequence as established until the foot (measured from the middle of the heel) measures 6.25 (7/7.5/8/8.75) in [16 (17.5/19/20.5/22) cm].

TOE DECREASES

Change color to Raw White and work paired banded toe decreases according to Basic instructions (see page 40).

FINISHING

Weave in all ends.

COLORWORK CHART A

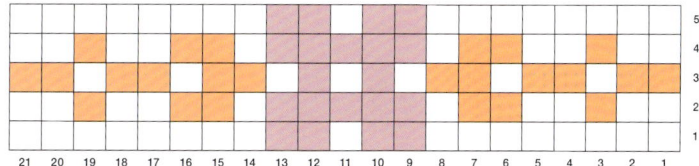

COLORWORK CHART B

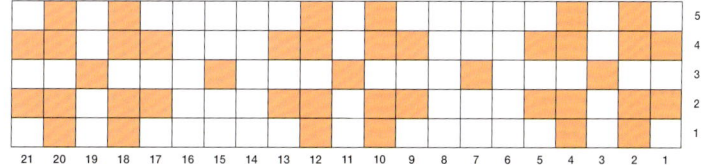

Taavi

SIZES
W5½/6 (W7/8, W9/9½ [M7/7½], W11/12 [M8½/9], M10/11)

MATERIALS
Lana Grossa Meilenweit 100 Tweed: 80% wool, 20% polyamide/nylon; 459 yd (420 m) per 3.5 oz (100 g)

- Light Beige 169: 1 skein

Lana Grossa Meilenweit 100: 80% wool, 20% polyamide/nylon; 459 yd (420 m) per 3.5 oz (100 g)

- Orange 1384: 1 skein

DPN set in US size 2 (2.5–3.0 mm) (or other preferred needle type, see page 10)

Cable needle

Stitch markers

Tapestry needle

Scissors

GAUGE
In stockinette stitch with US size 2 needles (2.5–3.0 mm):

28 sts and 40 rows = 4 x 4 in (10 x 10 cm)

BASIC PATTERN
STOCKINETTE STITCH
In rows: Knit on RS, purl on WS.
In rounds: Knit all stitches in all rounds.

CONSTRUCTION
The sock is worked from the cuff down, featuring a cabled cuff, a boomerang heel, and paired banded toe decreases. The larger colorwork pattern is worked with two strands of yarn held together around the leg, and a second smaller colorwork pattern is worked before the toe decreases.

INSTRUCTIONS

CUFF

CO 60 (60/66/66/66) sts in Orange, distribute sts onto 4 DPNs [= 15–15–15–15 (15–15–15–15/16–16–17–17/16–16–17–17/16–16–17–17) sts per needle], and join to work in the round.

Rounds 1–4: *Knit 4, purl 2*, repeat from * to * continuously.

Round 5: *Hold 2 sts on cable needle in front of work, knit 2, knit 2 from cn, purl 2*, repeat from * to * continuously.

Rounds 6–9: *Knit 4, purl 2*, repeat from * to * continuously.

Round 10: *Hold 2 sts on cable needle in front of work, knit 2, knit 2 from cn, purl 2*, repeat from * to * continuously.

Rounds 11–14: *Knit 4, purl 2*, repeat from * to * continuously.

SIZES W9/9½ [M7/7½], W11/12 [M8½/9]

In the first round after the cuff, decrease 2 sts, evenly spaced [= 64 sts].

SIZE M10/11

In the first round after the cuff, increase 2 sts, evenly spaced [= 68 sts].

LEG

Change color to Light Beige, and work 3 rounds in stockinette stitch.

SIZES W5½/6 AND W7/8

In Round 4: *K12, pm*, repeat from * to * 4 times more.

SIZES W9/9½ [M7/7½], W11/12 [M8½/9]

In Round 4: K12, *pm, k1, pm, k12*, repeat from * to * 3 times more.

SIZE M10/11

In Round 4: k12, pm, k2, pm, k12, pm, k1, pm, k12, pm, k2, pm, k12, pm, k1, pm, k12, pm, k2, pm.

In the next 7 rounds, work Colorwork Chart A with two strands of Orange held together between markers all around.

Work 39 rounds in stockinette stitch.

HEEL

Work a boomerang heel in Orange over the 30 (30/32/32/34) sts of needles 4 and 1 according to Basic instructions (see page 36).

FOOT

Change color to Light Beige, and work stockinette stitch in the round.

After having worked 5.5 (6/6.75/7.25/8) in [14 (15.5/17/18.5/20) cm] (measured from the middle of the heel), k16 (16/16/16/18), pm, work Colorwork Chart B with two strands of Orange held together over 28 (28/32/32/32) sts widthwise, pm, k16 (16/16/16/18).

In the next 2 rounds, continue the colorwork pattern over the 28 (28/32/32/32) stitches on the top of the foot.

Continue, working stockinette stitch in Light Beige until the foot (measured from the middle of the heel) measures 6.25 (7/7.5/8/8.75) in [16 (17.5/19/20.5/22) cm].

TOE DECREASES

Change color to Orange, and work paired banded toe decreases according to Basic instructions (see page 40).

FINISHING

Weave in all ends.

COLORWORK CHART A

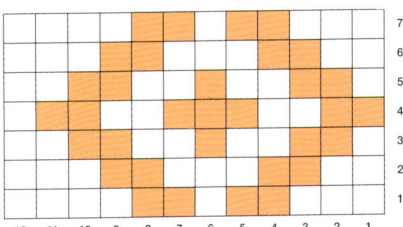

COLORWORK CHART B

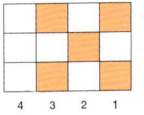

Janek

SIZES
W5½/6 (W7/8, W9/9½ [M7/7½], W11/12 [M8½/9], M10/11)

MATERIALS
Lana Grossa Meilenweit 50 Cashmere: 70% wool, 25% polyamide/nylon, 5% cashmere; 230 yd (210 m) per 1.8 oz (50 g)
- Brillant Blue 16: 2 skeins

Lana Grossa Meilenweit 100: 80% wool, 20% polyamide/nylon; 459 yd (420 m) per 3.5 oz (100 g)
- Light Heather Grey 1358: 1 skein

DPN set in US size 2 (2.5–3.0 mm) (or other preferred needle type, see page 10)

Stitch markers

Tapestry needle

Scissors

GAUGE
In stockinette stitch with US size 2 needles (2.5–3.0 mm):
30 sts and 40 rows = 4 x 4 in (10 x 10 cm)

BASIC PATTERN
STOCKINETTE STITCH
In rows: Knit on RS, purl on WS.
In rounds: Knit all stitches in all rounds.

CUFF RIBBING
2x2 ribbing: *Knit 2, purl 2*, repeat from * to * continuously.

CONSTRUCTION
The sock is worked from the cuff down, featuring a boomerang heel and paired banded toe decreases. The colorwork motif is worked with two strands of yarn held together on the top of the foot.

INSTRUCTIONS

CUFF

CO 60 (60/64/64/68) sts in Brillant Blue, distribute sts evenly onto 4 DPNs [= 15 (15/16/16/17) sts per needle], and join to work in the round.

Work 15 rounds [= 1.5 in (3.5 cm)] in cuff ribbing.

LEG

Knit all stitches, until the leg (measured from cast-on edge) measures 6.25 in (16 cm).

HEEL

Work a boomerang heel according to Basic instructions (see page 36) in stockinette stitch over the 30 (30/32/32/34) sts of needles 4 and 1.

FOOT

Work stockinette stitch in the round.

After having worked 3 (3.25/3.75/4/4.25) in [8 (8.5/9.5/10/11) cm] (measured from the middle of the heel), continue as follows:

K21 (21/23/23/25), pm, k19, pm, k20 (20/22/22/24).

In the next 19 rounds, work the colorwork motif with two strands of Light Heather Grey held together over the 19 sts between the markers.

Change to Brillant Blue and continue until the foot (measured from the middle of the heel) measures 6.25 (7/7.5/8/8.75) in [16 (17.5/19/20.5/22) cm].

TOE DECREASES

Finish by working paired banded toe decreases according to Basic instructions (see page 40).

FINISHING

Weave in all ends.

COLORWORK CHART

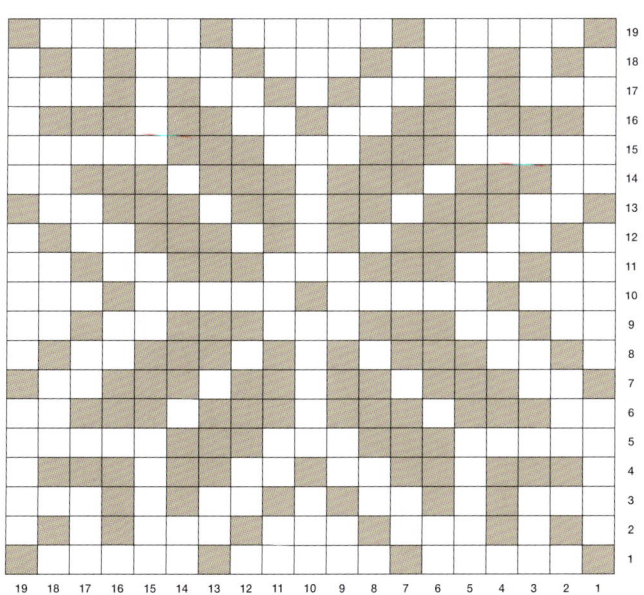

Lisette

SIZES
W5½/6 (W7/8, W9/9½ [M7/7½], W11/12 [M8½/9], M10/11)

MATERIALS
Lana Grossa Meilenweit 100: 80% wool, 20% polyamide/nylon; 459 yd (420 m) per 3.5 oz (100 g)
- Bordeaux 1380: 1 skein
- Light Blue 1364: 1 skein

Lana Grossa Meilenweit 100 Seta: 55% wool, 25% polyamide/nylon, 20% silk; 437 yd (400 m) per 3.5 oz (100 g)
- Raspberry Red 33: 1 skein

Lana Grossa Meilenweit 100 Tweed: 80% wool, 20% polyamide/nylon; 459 yd (420 m) per 3.5 oz (100 g)
- Mustard Yellow 157: 1 skein

DPN set in US size 2 (2.5–3.0 mm) (or other preferred needle type, see page 10)

Stitch markers

Tapestry needle

Scissors

GAUGE
In stockinette stitch with US size 2 needles (2.5–3.0 mm):
30 sts and 42 rows = 4 x 4 in (10 x 10 cm)

BASIC PATTERN
STOCKINETTE STITCH
In rows: Knit on RS, purl on WS.
In rounds: Knit all stitches in all rounds.

CUFF RIBBING
2x2 ribbing: *Knit 2, purl 2*, repeat from * to * continuously.

CONSTRUCTION
The sneaker sock is worked from the toe up, featuring a boomerang heel and ending with a short ribbed cuff. The colorwork motif is worked with two strands of yarn held together on the top of the foot.

INSTRUCTIONS

TOE INCREASES

For the toe section, using Bordeaux and long-tail cast-on for toe-up socks (see page 42), CO 8 sts.

Work increases until you have a total of 60 (60/64/64/68) sts on the needles [= 15 (15/16/16/17) sts per needle].

FOOT

Work stockinette stitch in the round over all sts until piece has reached a length of approx. 3 (3.25/3.75/4/4.25) in [7.5 (8.5/9.5/10/11) cm] (measured from toe section).

In the next round, k18 (18/20/20/22), pm, k25, pm, k17 (17/19/19/21).

In the next 25 rounds, work the colorwork motif over the 25 sts between the markers with two strands each held together in colors Light Blue, Raspberry Red, and Mustard Yellow, respectively.

After having completed Round 25 of the colorwork chart, remove the markers, and work all stitches in stockinette stitch.

HEEL

After having worked 6.25 (7/7.5/8/8.75) in [16 (17.5/19/20.5/22) cm] (measured from the tip of the toe), begin working a boomerang heel according to Basic instructions (see page 36) in stockinette stitch over the 30 (30/32/32/34) sts of needles 4 and 1.

LEG

After having completed the boomerang heel, work 10 rounds in stockinette stitch.

CUFF

Work 6 rounds in cuff ribbing pattern.

Bind off all stitches loosely as they appear (knit stitches in knit and purl stitches in purl), making sure the opening does not turn out too tight.

FINISHING

Weave in all ends.

COLORWORK CHART

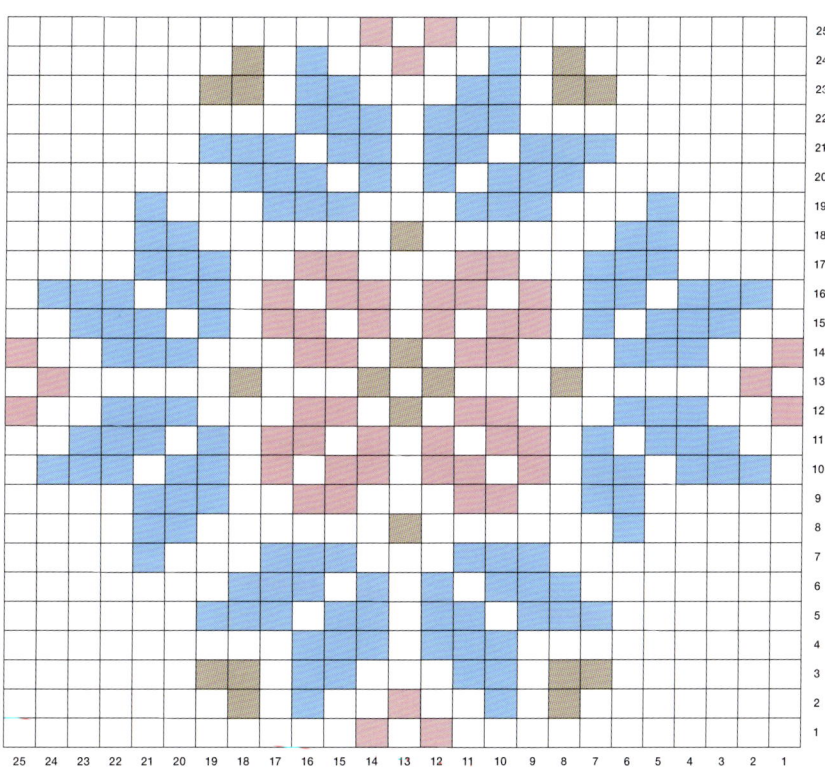

Anneli

SIZES
W5½/6 (W7/8, W9/9½ [M7/7½], W11/12 [M8½/9], M10/11)

MATERIALS
Lana Grossa Meilenweit 100 Seta: 55% wool, 25% polyamide/nylon, 20% silk; 437 yd (400 m) per 3.5 oz (100 g)

- Clay Red 27: 1 skein

Lana Grossa Meilenweit 100 Merino Extrafine: 75% Merino wool, 25% polyamide/nylon; 459 yd (420 m) per 3.5 oz (100 g)

- Lilac 2435: 1 skein

Lana Grossa Cool Wool 4 Socks: 75% Merino wool, 25% polyamide/nylon; 459 yd (420 m) per 3.5 oz (100 g)

- Jeans Blue 7704: 1 skein

DPN set in US size 2 (2.5–3.0 mm) (or other preferred needle type, see page 10)

Stitch markers

Tapestry needle

Scissors

GAUGE
In stockinette stitch with US size 2 needles (2.5–3.0 mm):
30 sts and 42 rows = 4 x 4 in (10 x 10 cm)

BASIC PATTERN
STOCKINETTE STITCH
In rows: Knit on RS, purl on WS.
In rounds: Knit all stitches in all rounds.

CUFF RIBBING
2x2 ribbing: *Knit 2, purl 2*, repeat from * to * continuously.

CONSTRUCTION
The sock is worked from the cuff down, featuring a boomerang heel and paired banded toe decreases, as well as two different colorwork patterns, each worked with two strands of yarn held together all around the leg during the striped sections.

INSTRUCTIONS

CUFF

CO 60 (60/64/64/68) sts in Lilac, distribute sts evenly onto 4 DPNs [= 15 (15/16/16/17) sts per needle], and join to work in the round.

Work 15 rounds [= 1.5 in (3.5 cm)] in cuff ribbing.

LEG

SIZES W5½/6, W7/8

Change color to Clay Red.

Work 6 rounds in stockinette stitch.

Change color to Jeans Blue.

Work 2 rounds in stockinette stitch.

In the next 4 rounds, holding two strands of Lilac together, work Colorwork Chart A all around.

Work 2 rounds in stockinette stitch.

Change color to Clay Red.

Work 4 rounds in stockinette stitch.

Change color to Lilac.

Work 3 rounds in stockinette stitch.

In the next 6 rounds, holding two strands of Jeans Blue together, work Colorwork Chart B all around.

Work 3 rounds in stockinette stitch.

Change color to Clay Red.

Work 4 rounds in stockinette stitch.

Change color to Jeans Blue.

Work 2 rounds in stockinette stitch.

In the next 4 rounds, holding two strands of Lilac together, work Colorwork Chart A all around.

Work 2 rounds in stockinette stitch.

Change color to Clay Red.

Work 8 rounds in stockinette stitch.

SIZES W9/9½ [M7/7½], W11/12 [M8½/9]

Work Colorwork Chart A and all color changes as described for the smaller sizes.

For Colorwork Chart B, the number of stitches available in the round and the number of stitches in the colorwork motif don't match. When working these sizes, you might want to shift the pattern so the spot with extra stitches without colorwork ends up on the interior side of the leg.

To do this, work as follows:

For the left sock: 48 sts according to Colorwork Chart B, 4 sts plain without colorwork, 12 sts according to Colorwork Chart B.

For the right sock: 12 sts according to Colorwork Chart B, 4 sts plain without colorwork, 48 sts according to Colorwork Chart B.

SIZE M10/11

Work Colorwork Chart A and all color changes as described for the smaller sizes.

For Colorwork Chart B, the number of stitches available in the round and the number of stitches in the colorwork motif don't match. When working these sizes, you might want to shift the pattern so the spot with extra stitches without colorwork ends up on the interior side of the leg.

To do this, work as follows:

For the left sock: 48 sts according to Colorwork Chart B, 2 sts plain without colorwork, 18 sts according to Colorwork Chart B.

For the right sock: 18 sts according to Colorwork Chart B, 2 sts plain without colorwork, 48 sts according to Colorwork Chart B.

HEEL

Work a boomerang heel according to Basic instructions (see page 36) in Lilac in stockinette stitch over the 30 (30/32/32/34) sts of needles 4 and 1.

FOOT

Change color to Clay Red, and work all stitches in stockinette stitch until the foot (measured from the middle of the heel) measures 6.25 (7/7.5/8/8.75) in [16 (17.5/19/20.5/22) cm].

TOE DECREASES

In Lilac, work paired banded toe decreases according to Basic instructions (see page 40)

FINISHING

Weave in all ends.

COLORWORK CHART A

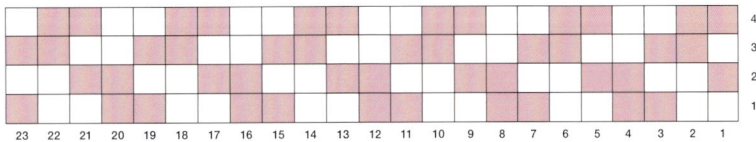

COLORWORK CHART B

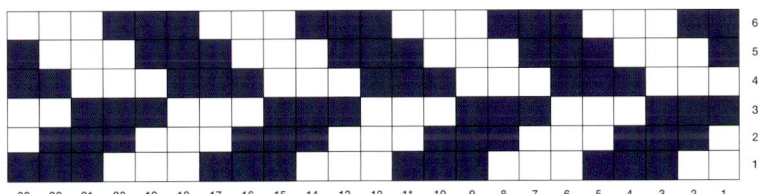

Rain

SIZES
W5½/6 (W7/8, W9/9½ [M7/7½], W11/12 [M8½/9], M10/11)

MATERIALS
Lana Grossa Cool Wool 4 Socks: 75% Merino wool, 25% polyamide/nylon; 459 yd (420 m) per 3.5 oz (100 g)
- Anthracite 7707: 1 skein

Lana Grossa Meilenweit 50 Cashmere: 70% wool, 25% polyamide/nylon, 5% cashmere; 230 yd (210 m) per 1.8 oz (50 g)
- Mint 28: 1 skein

DPN set in US size 2 (2.5–3.0 mm) (or other preferred needle type, see page 10)
Stitch markers
Cable needle
Tapestry needle
Scissors

GAUGE
In stockinette stitch with US size 2 needles (2.5–3.0 mm):
28 sts and 40 rows = 4 x 4 in (10 x 10 cm)

BASIC PATTERN
STOCKINETTE STITCH
In rows: Knit on RS, purl on WS.
In rounds: Knit all stitches in all rounds.

CONSTRUCTION
The sock is worked from the cuff down with a cabled cuff, a boomerang heel, and paired banded toe decreases. The colorwork pattern is worked with one strand of yarn in the striped sections of leg and foot.

INSTRUCTIONS

CUFF

CO 60 (60/66/66/66) sts in Mint, distribute sts onto 4 DPNs [= 15-15-15-15 (15-15-15-15/16-16-17-17/16-16-17-17/16-16-17-17) sts], and join to work in the round.

Rounds 1–5: *Knit 4, purl 2*, repeat from * to * continuously.

Round 6: *Hold 2 sts on cable needle in front of work, knit 2, knit 2 from cn, purl 2*, repeat from * to * continuously.

Rounds 7–11: *Knit 4, purl 2*, repeat from * to * continuously.

Round 12: *Hold 2 sts on cable needle in front of work, knit 2, knit 2 from cn, purl 2*, repeat from * to * continuously.

Rounds 13–16: *Knit 4, purl 2*, repeat from * to * continuously.

SIZES W9/9½ [M7/7½], W11/12 [M8½/9]

In the first round after the cuff, decrease 2 sts, evenly spaced [= 64 sts].

SIZE M10/11

In the first round after the cuff, increase 2 sts, evenly spaced [= 68 sts].

LEG

SIZES W5½/6, W7/8

Change color to Anthracite.

Work 2 rounds in stockinette stitch.

Change color to Mint.

Work 1 round in stockinette stitch.

Change color to Anthracite.

Work 1 round in stockinette stitch.

Change color to Mint.

Work 2 rounds in stockinette stitch.

In the next 11 rounds, work Colorwork Chart A with yarn held single all around.

Work 2 rounds in stockinette stitch.

Change color to Anthracite.

Work 1 round in stockinette stitch.

Change color to Mint.

Work 1 round in stockinette stitch.

Change color to Anthracite.

Work 28 rounds in stockinette stitch.

SIZES W9/9½ [M7/7½], W11/12 [M8½/9]

Work all color changes as described for sizes W5½/6, W7/8.

For Colorwork Chart A, the number of stitches available in the round and the number of stitches in the colorwork motif don't match. When working these sizes, you might want to shift the pattern so the spot with extra stitches without colorwork ends up on the interior side of the leg. To do this, work as follows:

For the left sock: Work stitches 1–12 of Colorwork Chart A four times widthwise [= 48 sts], work stitches 9–24 of Colorwork Chart A [= 16 sts] [= total of 64 sts].

For the right sock: Work stitches 1–16 of Colorwork Chart A [= 16 sts], work stitches 1–12 of Colorwork Chart A four times widthwise [= 48 sts] [= total of 64 sts].

SIZE M10/11

Work all color changes as described for sizes W5½/6, W7/8.

For Colorwork Chart A, the number of stitches available in the round and the number of stitches in the colorwork motif don't match. When working these sizes, you might want to shift the pattern so the spot with extra stitches without colorwork ends up on the interior side of the leg. To do this, work as follows:

For the left sock: Work stitches 1–12 of Colorwork Chart A three times widthwise [= 36 sts], work stitches 1–15 of Colorwork Chart A [= 15 sts], work stitches 8–24 of Colorwork Chart A [= 17 sts] [= total of 68 sts].

For the right sock: Work stitches 1–17 of Colorwork Chart A [= 17 sts], work stitches 10–12 of Colorwork Chart A [= 3 sts], work stitches 1–12 of Colorwork Chart A four times widthwise [= 48 sts] [= total of 68 sts].

HEEL

Work a boomerang heel according to Basic instructions (see page 36) in stockinette stitch over the 30 (30/32/32/34) sts of needles 4 and 1.

FOOT

Work in stockinette stitch until the foot (measured from the middle of the heel) measures 5 (5.75/6.25/7/7.5) in [13 (14.5/16/17.5/19) cm].

Change color to Mint.

Work 1 round in stockinette stitch.

Change color to Anthracite.

Work 1 round in stockinette stitch.

Change color to Mint.

Work 1 round in stockinette stitch.

In the next 5 rounds, work Colorwork Chart B with one strand of Anthracite all around.

Work 1 round in stockinette stitch.

Change color to Anthracite.

Work 1 round in stockinette stitch.

Change color to Mint.

Work 1 round in stockinette stitch.

The foot should now have a length (measured from the middle of the heel) of 6.25 (7/7.5/8/8.75) in [16 (17.5/19/20.5/22) cm]. If it is still shorter, change color to Anthracite and continue in stockinette stitch until the desired length has been reached.

SIZES W9/9½ [M7/7½], W11/12 [M8½/9], M10/11

For Colorwork Chart B, the number of stitches available in the round and the number of stitches in the colorwork motif don't match. Since the beginning of the round is located on the sole of the foot, further adjustment is not necessary.

TOE DECREASES

Work paired banded toe decreases (see page 40) in Anthracite.

FINISHING

Weave in all ends.

COLORWORK CHART A

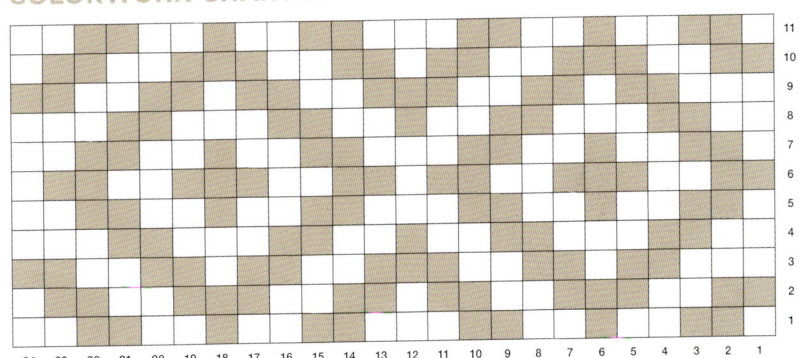

COLORWORK CHART B

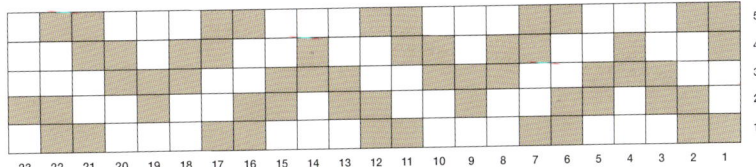

Talvi

SIZES
W5½/6 (W7/8, W9/9½ [M7/7½], W11/12 [M8½/9], M10/11)

MATERIALS
Lana Grossa Meilenweit 100 Seta: 55% wool, 25% polyamide/nylon, 20% silk; 437 yd (400 m) per 3.5 oz (100 g)

- Clay Brown 32: 1 skein

Lana Grossa Meilenweit 100 Merino Extrafine: 75% Merino wool, 25% polyamide/nylon; 459 yd (420 m) per 3.5 oz (100 g)

- Dark Fuchsia 2437: 1 skein

DPN set in US size 2 (2.5–3.0 mm) (or other preferred needle type, see page 10)

Stitch markers

Tapestry needle

Scissors

GAUGE
In stockinette stitch with US size 2 needles (2.5–3.0 mm):
28 sts and 40 rows = 4 x 4 in (10 x 10 cm)

BASIC PATTERN
STOCKINETTE STITCH
In rows: Knit on RS, purl on WS.
In rounds: Knit all stitches in all rounds.

CUFF RIBBING
2x2 ribbing: *Knit 2, purl 2*, repeat from * to * continuously.

TWISTED RIBBING PATTERN
Knit 1 through the back loop, purl 1, knit 1 through the back loop, purl 1, knit 1 through the back loop.

CONSTRUCTION
The sock is worked from the cuff down, featuring a boomerang heel and paired banded toe decreases. The colorwork pattern on the front of the sock is worked with two strands of yarn held together between two sections of twisted ribbing.

INSTRUCTIONS

CUFF

CO 60 (60/64/64/68) sts in Clay Brown, distribute sts evenly onto 4 DPNs [= 15 (15/16/16/17) sts per needle], and join to work in the round.

Work 12 rounds in cuff ribbing pattern.

LEG

Round 1: K19 (19/21/21/23), k1-tbl, p1, k1-tbl, p1, k1-tbl, k2, k8, k2, k1-tbl, p1, k1-tbl, p1, k1-tbl, k19 (19/21/21/23).

Round 2: Repeat Round 1.

Round 3: K19 (19/21/21/23), k1-tbl, p1, k1-tbl, p1, k1-tbl, k2, pm, k8, pm, k2, k1-tbl, p1, k1-tbl, p1, k1-tbl, k19 (19/21/21/23).

Round 4: Repeat Round 1, at the same time working the colorwork pattern with two strands of Dark Fuchsia held together over the 8 sts between the markers.

Repeat Round 4 until the leg (measured from cast-on edge) measures 6 in (15 cm).

HEEL

Work a boomerang heel according to Basic instructions (see page 36) in stockinette stitch over the 30 (30/32/32/34) sts of needles 4 and 1, and in intermittent rounds, continue the colorwork pattern on the front of the foot.

FOOT

Repeat Round 4 until the foot (measured from the middle of the heel) measures 6.25 (7/7.5/8/9) in [16 (17.5/19/20.5/22) cm].

TOE DECREASES

Finish by working paired banded toe decreases according to Basic instructions (see page 40).

FINISHING

Weave in all ends.

COLORWORK CHART

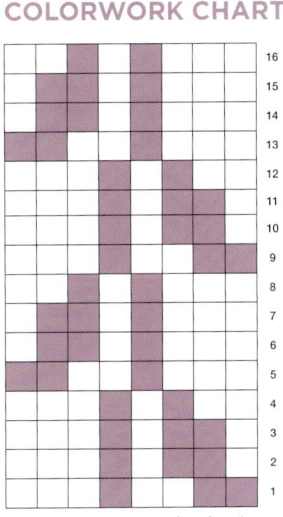

Talvi 123

Acknowledgments

The biggest thank you goes to my husband Marcel, who always supports me in everything I do and never tires of holding one skein of yarn next to another until we've found the perfect color combination together. I'm glad that there's a little bit of Marcel hidden somewhere in every one of my books!

I would like to thank my mom, my cousin Marie, and my chosen sister Pia for their feedback on my (until now secret) designs, which is very important to me. It's great that you're on board.

A great thank you to the entire team at EMF Verlag, especially my editor Melanie Kowalski, for their excellent cooperation and their trust in my imagination.

Many thanks to Lana Grossa for providing yarn support for this book in the form of the most beautiful fingering weight yarns in all colors and varieties.

About the Author

Sarah Prieur is one of the best-known representatives of the German-speaking crochet and knitting community and has more recently also established herself as a nonfiction author in the DIY sector. Now a Munich local by choice, the Rhineland native is married and, on her Instagram channel @sapri_design, not only takes her followers behind the scenes of her numerous handicraft projects but also shares her travels and everyday experiences with her audience. In her video podcast *Sarah's Needle Stories* on YouTube, she offers a close-up account of her private and professional projects. Her books, published by EMF Verlag, have been translated into numerous languages and range from the "Potterhead" knitting universe to crochet patterns for both little ones and grown-ups. Sarah's projects often reflect the motto, "Why buy when you can do it yourself and make it unique?" Individuality and the joy in handcrafting at the highest quality level are the basic principles of all her designs.